SHUNYA SAMPADANE

The Main Scripture of the Veerashaivas.

A concise composition.

Sixth Edition

Linga Raju, M. D.

SHUNYA SAMPADANE

[Śūnya Saṁpādane]

The Main Scripture of the Veerashaivas.
A concise composition.

Linga Raju

Revised March 2022

ISBN: 9781720193289

For our grandchildren

Vikram, Kyle, and Mila

TABLE OF CONTENTS

Introduction 9

Veerashaiva and Lingayata 11

Anubhava Mantapa 15

Vachana 19

Sharana *(Śaraṇa)* 21

Theistic Monism 24

Shunya Sampadane Texts 26

Shunya Sampadane and the Upanishads 32

Shunya *(Śūnya)* 37

The Divinity 42

Linga *(Liṅga)* 48

Prabhudēva's Shūnya Sampādane 54

The Creation 55

Introduction of Prabhudeva 58

Shatsthala *(Ṣaṭsthala)* 62

Piṇḍasthala 65

Piṇḍa-jñāna-sthala 68

Saṁsāraheyasthala 72

Māyāvilāsaviḍambana-sthala 75

Liṅgadhāraṇasthala 84

Bhaktasthala 89

Māheshvarasthala 93

Prasādisthala 96

Prāṇaliṅgisthala 99

Prāṇāyāma......106
Sharaṇasthala......110
Aikyasthala......115
Jaṅgamasthala......120
Muktāyakka's Sampādane......124
Siddharāmayya's Sampādane......130
The Legendary Story of Siddharamayya....130
Philosophical Discussion......132
The Sampādane Concerning the Grace Bestowed by Basavaṇṇa upon Chennabasavaṇṇa......146
Basavaṇṇa......146
Grace bestowed by Basavaṇṇa upon Chennabasavaṇṇa......155
Sampādane dealing with Prabhudēva's arrival at the city of Kalyāṇa......162
Sampādane of Maruḷushaṅkaradēva......171
Basaveshvara's Sampādane......174
Chennabasaveshvara's Sampādane......182
Chennabasavaṇṇa......182
Chennabasavaṇṇa's Sampādane......184
Maḍivāḷayya's Sampādane......193
Siddharāmayya's Bestowal of Grace by the Guru......198
Prabhudēva's Apotheosis......204
Āydakki Mārayya's Sampādane......209
Mārayya and his wife Lakkamma......210
Mōḷigayya's Sampādane......220

Kashmir King and his Wife 220
Oneness of Husband and Wife 228
Nuliya Chandayya's Sampādane 238
Ghaṭṭivāḷayya's Sampādane 245
Mahādēviyakka's Sampādane 250
Akka Mahādēvi 250
Sampadane of Akka Mahādēvi 253
Sampādane of Prabhudēva's Tour and Return 289
Sampādane of Prabhudēva's Ascension on the Throne of the Absolute 293
Prabhudēva's Feast 296
Prophecy of the Sharaṇas' End 301
Gōraksha's Sampadane, and all Saints' Aikya 307
Concluding remarks in Shunya Sampadane 321
References 323

INTRODUCTION

Shunya Sampadane (Śūnya Saṁpādane) means attainment of Shunya, the Absolute State (see article 'Shunya' that comes later on in this book). Some have translated 'Shūnya Saṁpādane' to mean 'Acquisition of Nothing'.

The term 'Shunya Sampadane' is also applied for the text compiled in the form of a document or a book with a title of Shunya Sampadane. **Shunya Sampadane describes the process of attainment of the absolute 'Shunya' by various Sharanas** (Sharana article comes later on in this book).

The term ***'Shunya (Śūnya)'*** is pronounced with a long vowel 'u'. The sound of pronunciation of any long vowel is held for twice the duration of time of that of the short vowel. The letter 's' at the beginning is a palatal sibilant where the sound is produced with the tongue almost touching the palate (roof of the mouth) and represented as 'sh'. Thus, Shunya can be written as Shuunya. Shunya is sometimes written as 'Shoonya' also.

The term ***'Sampadane (Saṁpādane)'*** has three 'a' vowels. Of these, the first and the third vowels are short vowels whereas the second/middle 'a' is a long vowel. The letter 's' at the beginning is a dental sibilant where the sound is produced with the tongue almost touching the back of the upper teeth and represented only as 's'. Thus Shunya Sampadane can be written as 'Shuunya Sampaadane'.

The Shūnya Saṁpādane text is one of the most important documents of the Veerashaiva philosophy and practice, and it occupies a very high place in the whole range of Indian literature (1).

Veerashaiva and Lingayata

The two most important aspects of Veerashaivism are ***Lingadhāraṇe*** which is the investiture of Linga by a Guru to a disciple, and the ***Shaṭsthala*** system of practice which is the spiritual hierarchy of six stages through which the seeker rises stage by stage till the apparent duality vanishes and the attainment of oneness occurs. If both these two components are not there, then it is not Veerashaivism. (2).

It is generally accepted that the present day Veerashaivas *(Vīraśaiva)* and Lingayatas *(Liṅgāyata)* are the followers of the Sharana *(Śaraṇa)* Philosophy and Practices put forward in the Kannaḍa vachanas of Basavaṇṇa and his contemporaries of the twelfth century of Common Era (CE/AD).

The term 'Veerashaiva' is also depicted as 'Virasaiva'. The 'i' is a long vowel represented as 'ee'. And the 's' is a palatal sibilant where the sound is produced with the tongue almost touching the palate (roof of the mouth) and represented as 'sh'.

- The term 'Veerashaiva' as well as the practicing Veerashaivas existed prior to the 12th century, but their philosophy and practices were based on the Veerashaiva parts of the Shivagamas (9th century) and/or Siddhanta Shikhamani (10th century). Both these scriptures are in Sanskrit.

- Then in the Sanskrit commentary on Brahma-sutras called 'Srikarabhashya', Sripatipandita stated that **Veerashaiva doctrine is 'Visheshaadvaita'** and that the Veerashaiva Philosophy is same as that in the Upanishads. He referred to Shivagamas and Siddhanta Shikhamani, but did not refer to Basavanna and his contemporary Sharaṇas of the twelfth century. Sripatipandita of Srikarabhashya belonged to the eleventh century around 1070 CE.
- Then the twelfth century Sharanas revitalized the Veerashaiva Faith.
- Most practicing Veerashaivas became the followers of the Sharana Philosophy.
- Some Veerashaivas continued their previously practiced faith based on the Shivagamas and /or Siddhanta Shikhamani.
- The Veerashaiva Faith, remained somewhat obscure until the 15th century when it was revived under the Vijayanagara Empire. The revived Veerashaivas are the followers of the Sharana Philosophy.
- Most of the present day Veerashaivas are the followers of this revived Sharana Philosophy.
- Some who call themselves Veerashaivas continue to practice their faith based on Shivagamas, Siddhanta Shikhamani, and/or Shrikarabhashya.
- Practice of some Veerashaivas, seems to be based on the combination of Sharana Philosophy and the Philosophy that is in one or more of the Sanskrit scriptures listed above.

- The term 'Lingayata' is pronounced with a long vowel 'a' as 'Lingaayata'. It does not come in any literature prior to the 12th century. The origin of the word Lingayata is not only obscure but also conspicuously absent in religious literature.
- Shunya Sampadane (1) states ***'When the faith in the Ishtalinga obtained through the Guru's grace grows, the Ishtalinga becomes Āyatalinga'.*** Shunya Sampadane interprets *'Āyata'* as *'what is come'* in the vachanas. Thus, Āyatalinga means *'what is come is Linga'.* By rearranging the two parts of the term 'Āyata-Linga' in reverse, one can see that it becomes 'Linga-ayata' - Lingaayata.
- The term Lingayata was used for its literal meaning in a few vachanas of the Sharanas. During the Linga initiation ceremony, the Guru places the Ishtalinga on the palm of the disciple, and says 'Lingayata'. The meaning of the term Lingayata is said to be 'Linga comes (to the disciple who has developed deep faith and is longing for it)'.
- The term Lingayata was not applicable to the practitioners of the Sharana Philosophy then.
- The term Lingayata was not used for the term Veerashaiva even in the 15th through 17th centuries CE, let alone in the 12th century.
- It seems that the use of the term Lingayata for the practitioners of Sharana Philosophy came to vogue sometime more recently than the 17th century CE.

- The terms 'Veerashaiva' and 'Lingayata' have been used interchangeably. Further, the terms 'Veerashaivism' and 'Lingāyatism' are also used interchangeably.
- However, it is to be noted that some who call themselves Veerashaivas, do not want to be called Liṅgāyatas.
- In the Sharaṇa Philosophy, the emphasis has shifted from Shiva to Liṅga. The Philosophy and Practice of the Sharaṇas is all about Liṅga.

Anubhava Mantapa

Anubhava Maṇṭapa was an Academy of Philosophers, Scholars, and Mystics. It was a sacred, spiritual, religious, and social academy. It was established by Basavaṇṇa in the twelfth century CE, in the city of Kalyāṇa which is in the present day Karnāṭaka State, India. Anubhava Maṇṭapa has also been called as *'Anubhava Gōṣṭhi'*. Sometimes it is referred to as an *'Academy of the Sharaṇas'* or the *'Assembly of Sharaṇas'*.

Simple meaning of *'Anubhava'* is experience. *'Anubhāva'*, with a long vowel 'ā' in it, has a deeper meaning. It is to rouse the powers latent in the innermost core of the heart and to rise to a direct experience of the Divine Reality. 'Anubhāva' is Realization of the Divine enshrined in one's own heart through Self-experience. The Realization is through inner intuition which transcends the reach of mind and intellect. But this experience of the Divine should not be the monopoly of a chosen few. (1, 2).

In the twelfth century, religion itself had deteriorated into another means of exploitation, perpetuating social inequality and ignorance of spiritual truth. The time seemed right for a drastic reform. Basavaṇṇa started a movement to reform Veerashaivism from within. His efforts were mostly oriented in two directions – religion and society. He saw no difference between rich and poor, and between man and woman; he saw no difference among different castes; and he embedded this principle of equality among all in the religion. (1).

Basavaṇṇa did not want to lay down the law in matters of religion and philosophy. Thus came the existence of the Anubhava Maṇṭapa where a large number of philosophers, mystics, scholars and seekers would gather to participate in learned discussions. They came from all parts of the Indian subcontinent. Kalyāṇa was both a symbol and an actual place where the Anubhava Maṇṭapa became a sacred spiritual, religious and social academy. (1).

Basavaṇṇa, after having started this great Academy, had grown in spiritual progress. But as his work expanded, the problems too increased. Basavaṇṇa needed a luminous personality to carry out the task. It was at this time, as if answering Basavaṇṇa's inner call, Allama Prabhu, popularly known as Prabhudēva, arrived at Kalyāṇa. At the first encounter of Bhakta Basavaṇṇa and Jaṅgama Prabhudēva, Basavaṇṇa, after realizing the magnitude of Prabhudēva, surrenders to him in all humility, and requests Prabhudēva to lend him support in his work. Prabhudēva accepts the principal responsibility of the Anubhava Maṇṭapa; this gives a new vigor to their deliberations. (1).

There was a great need for a leader like Prabhudēva. Basavaṇṇa was too modest and unassuming. Prabhudēva's presence gave Basavaṇṇa courage and strength. It gave a direct and decisive blow, as it were, to traditionalists who opposed Basavaṇṇa, as well as to hypocrites in his own camp who paraded as great Sharaṇas. Prabhudēva was the central character, or protagonist – its moving spirit. He was regarded as the most intellectual of all the Veerashaiva scholars at the time. As he traveled all over India, he drew the scholars and the seekers towards Kalyāṇa. Prabhudēva presided over the discourses that were held in the Anubhava Maṇṭapa. (1).

The main theme of these discussions was the **Shaṭsthala** philosophy – Shaṭsthala is the spiritual hierarchy of six stages through which the seeker rises stage by stage till the apparent duality vanishes and attainment of oneness occurs. A new Philosophical System was developed, and with accurate interpretation, practical implementation of the idea was carried out. With this system, **the vachana literature was popularized by the Sharaṇas.** (1).

As president of the Anubhava Maṇṭapa, Prabhudēva proved to be the great Light that dispelled all doubts and difficulties. All these deliberations were documented in writing in the vachana form. **Anubhava Maṇṭapa was a tremendous source of these vachanas.** The vachanas were simple in form, and were in everyday language of the people. They were very inspirational and appealing to the masses. They were full of spiritual insight and had mystic overtones. The vachanas were said to be comparable to the Upanishadic sayings of the great ancient sages. The vachanas were used for propagating spiritual knowledge and the right way of life among the masses. (1).

The city of Kalyāṇa, now called Basava Kalyāṇa is located in the northeastern corner part of Karnāṭaka, close to the border with Maharashtra State. An assembly hall has been built there where the Anubhava Maṇṭapa supposedly was. Basavaṇṇa's standing portrait (with Kūḍala Saṅgama background) is mounted on a dais consisting of six semi-circular stages decreasing in size from the base to the top, representing six stages of Shaṭsthala. There does not seem to be a representation of Shūnya-siṁhāsana (the throne of the Absolute) of Prabhudēva. This information is as of January 2010. (2).

Vachana

'Vachana *(vaĉana)*' is a Kannada word; it literally means 'that which is said' or 'that which is spoken'. **Vachana is a rhythmic prose.** Vachanas were widely used by this common religious faith to propagate knowledge and the right way of life among the masses. These vachanas are in the Kannada language, the language of the local people of Karnataka.

As to the pronunciation of the word 'vachana', all the three 'a' vowels are short vowels, 'c' is a palatal consonant where the sound is produced with the tongue almost touching the palate (roof of the mouth) and represented as 'ch', and 'n' is a dental consonant where the sound is produced with the tongue almost touching the back of the upper teeth.

In a span of twenty years' time then, an enormous number of vachanas were composed and recorded on palm leaves and metal plates. However, due to disturbed conditions that ensued, the vachana literature was scattered, and some of it was lost. (The disturbed situation is described in the 'Basavaṇṇa' article.)

During the Vijayanagara Empire in the 15th century, Veerashaiva scholars systematically collected the retrievable portions of the vachana literature, and compiled some of these vachanas into the form of a scripture known as Shunya Sampadane (1).

The Ganaka Vachana Samputa reference (3), lists 220 authors of vachanas including 54 unknown authors, and lists the number of vachanas they authored. The total number there comes to 20,144 vachanas: There are 1426 vachanas of Basavanna, 1645 vachanas of Allama Prabhudeva, 354 vachanas of Akka Mahadevi, 1792 vachanas of Chennabasavanna, 1679 vachanas of Siddharamayya, and many vachanas of other authors.

Vachana literature of Basavanna and his contemporary philosophers of the twelfth century is the basic scripture of the present day Veerashaivas. 'Vachanas', by default, refer to the vachanas of the 12th century Sharanas.

Although the vachana literature of the twelfth century Sharanas is the basic scripture, Shunya Sampadane is considered as the main scripture of the Veerashaivas. This is mainly because of the way the vachanas are presented in Shunya Sampadane in the form of discourses that occurred at the Academy of the Sharanas (Anubhava Mantapa) among the various 12th century Sharanas.

Sharana *(Śaraṇa)*

The readers may very well know that the term 'Sharana' comes very frequently in the vachanas. But sometimes it gets to be confusing because the term 'Sharana' is used in the vachanas to mean different things under different circumstances.

As to the pronunciation of the term 'Sharana (Śaraṇa)', all the three 'a' vowels are short vowels, the 's' at the beginning of the word is a palatal sibilant where the sound is produced with the tongue almost touching the palate (roof of the mouth) and represented as 'sh', and 'n' is a retroflex or cerebral – the sound is produced with the tongue bent backwards.

The meaning of the Kannada word *'Sharana'* is ***'one who submits oneself'.*** The gender of the word *'Sharana'* is male. The word *'Sharane'* represents the female gender. But in general, the term 'Sharana' is used for both genders.

Sharana refers to a person who diligently follows the philosophy and practices put forward in the vachanas of Basavanna and his contemporaries of the 12th century.

However, it seems that the term 'Sharana' is used exclusively to refer to Basavanna and his contemporaries who were spiritually advanced and were in the City of Kalyana at the time.

Karmic load is the accumulated karma from actions/deeds performed in the past life, and as a consequence, one enjoys the fruits of good deeds and suffers as a result of bad deeds. This does not apply to the Sharanas. **Sharana is free from such karmic body.** Sharana, though is in this world, is not of it. Sharana is above the nature of the body. Sharana is not the one who enjoys rewards set forth in the Agamas. (1).

Allama Prabhudeva uses the term 'Sharana' in his vachanas that are related to the creation:

'In the beginning there was nothing, not even Shunya (Void) or Nisshunya (Primal Void or non-Void). Then Sharana arose.'

This 'Sharana', used in this context, is the Eternal Being, the Knowledge, the Consciousness, the Ātman, or the Brahman.

Sharana is also a person who, in the person's spiritual progress, has completed the stage of **Sharanasthala** and has become a Sharana.

As the readers may very well know, Sharanasthala is the fifth of the six stages of **Shatsthala.** The Shatsthala is the most important spiritual doctrine and religious practice of the Sharanas.

This Sharana is spiritually advanced in that respect, and is the one who is characterized by pure delight (Ānanda) derived from contemplation on the inner Linga/Self.

Thus, it can be stated that:

- Sharana is steadfast in his moral code of conduct.
- Sharana is virtuous.
- Sharana has no desires.
- Sharana has no merits or demerits from the deeds performed. (Sharana has no 'karma', and does not have a karmic body.)
- Sharana is wise and does not have a tainted mind.
- And Sharana does not have any pride of caste, self, wealth, learning, and such.
- Sharana is a spiritually advanced person.

Theistic Monism

Veerashaiva Philosophy is Theistic Monism. Monism refers to a view that 'Reality' is basically one. The Reality encompasses the whole universe and everything else in it, including the worldly existence.

Atheism is a belief that there is no God, and theism is a belief in the existence of a God or Gods. Monotheism, then, is a belief that there is only one God, but that does not necessarily mean that there is only one Reality. Monotheism could imply duality, meaning that there are two Realities - referring to the belief that God and the individual are two separate and distinct entities. Thus, monotheism is not monism.

If the monists believe that this one Reality encompassing everything, is God, then that belief would be Theistic Monism. It is the belief that all is God and the Self is God (4).

In the Oneness System of Theistic Monism, the Reality has three categories (5):

- The Immanent Reality is the phenomenal universe. It is the abode of all living beings. It serves as a divinely devised training ground where, through pain and pleasure, and through life and death, all beings are driven to evolve in the Divinity.
- The Transcendental Reality contains, controls, and governs the Immanent Reality. All

worship and adoration are offered to this Reality. It bestows emancipation to those who perfect themselves.

- The substratum of these two categories of Reality is The Absolute Reality which is considered as Pure Consciousness. This Reality cannot be worshipped directly, but the goal of human life is to dissolve one's individuality into this Absolute Reality.

The Sanskrit term *'Advaita'* means 'non-duality'. The basic meaning of Advaitism is the non-duality of Ātman and Brahman. Ātman is pronounced with a long vowel 'a' as 'Aatman'; it is the individual-Self. Brahman is the universal-Self. Ātman and Brahman is one and the same.

The term 'Advaitism' when used in its strictest sense, only negates duality – negates everything conceivable or expressible. But the term 'Monism' means predicating one positive thing or oneness. Even so, in general, the term Monism is used in the English literature to mean Advaitism.

SHUNYA SAMPADANE TEXTS

Shunya Sampadane means attainment of Shunya, the Absolute State. Here in this article the term 'Shunya Sampadane' refers to the text of the vachanas compiled in the form of a document or a book with a title of Shunya Sampadane.

This Shunya Sampadane text is one of the most important documents of the Veerashaiva philosophy and faith, and it occupies a very high place in the whole range of Indian literature (1).

The pronunciation of 'Shunya Sampadane' is given under 'Introduction'.

Anubhava Mantapa, the Academy of Sharanas, was founded by Basavanna and was presided over by Allama Prabhudeva. Philosophers and Scholars from all over Indian subcontinent participated in this Academy. Discourses concerning religion and society were held there. These discourses were recorded as vachanas.

The vachanas that came out of the discussions at the Academy of the Sharanas bring out the Philosophy and practices of Veerashaivas. These vachanas of discussion among the great philosophers, particularly between Allama Prabhudeva and others at the Academy, clearly provide information about the Veerashaiva Philosophy and practice. Shunya Sampadane has these vachanas.

During the Vijayanagara Empire in the fifteenth century, the Veerashaiva scholars systematically collected the retrievable portions of the vachana literature, and compiled some of these vachanas of discussion, into the form of a scripture known as Shunya Sampadane (1). This was said to have been done under the patronage of Jakkanarya and Lakkanna Dondesha Ministers of Praudha Devaraya, or Devaraya II (1419 -1447 CE).

Over a period of time since the compilation of the first Shunya Sampadane in the fifteenth century, three more, to a total of four versions of Shunya Sampadane have been compiled:

- The first version was compiled by Shivagana Prasadi Mahadevayya. It comprises of 1012 vachanas.
- The second version containing 1599 vachanas was compiled by Halageyadeva.
- The third was prepared by Gummalapura Siddalingesha Shivayogi, a disciple of Tontada Siddalingeshvara. It contains 1439 vachanas.
- The fourth compilation of Shunya Sampadane with 1543 vachanas was by Gulura Siddhaveeranarya.
- The fourth version of Shunya Sampadane was compiled in the later part of the sixteenth century.

The fourth version was first edited and brought out in print form by Dr. P. G. Halakatti in the year 1930, and it was later revised and published by Professor S. S. Bhusanurmath in 1958. This Kannada version of the Shunya Sampadane was translated into a comprehensive edition in English by the Karnataka University, Dharwad, India.

This English composition by the Karnataka University, contains not only Kannada texts and vachanas but also English introduction, text, transliteration, translation, notes, and comments. The five volumes of Shunya Sampadane were published one at a time:

- Volume I edited by Dr. S. C. Nandimath, Professor L. M. A. Menezes and Dr. R. C. Hiremath was published in 1965.
- Volumes II, III and IV edited by Professor S. S. Bhoosnurmath and Professor Armando Menezes were published in 1968, 1969 and 1970 respectively.
- Volume V edited by Dr. M. S. Sunkapur and Professor Armando Menezes was published in 1972.
- This five volume version of Shunya Sampadane (1) is the one that is referred to in this article.

Author of the Fourth Version

The author of the fourth version of Shunya Sampadane, as stated above, was Shri Gulura Siddhavīraṇārya who was also called as Siddhavīrēshvara and Siddhavīrāchārya. His Guru was Bolabasavesha, and the Guru's Guru was the great Guru Tōṇṭada Siddhalingeshvara who was also the Guru of the third Shunya Sampadane composer Gommaḷāpura Siddhaliṅgēsa Shivayogi (also called Siddhaliṅgadēvaru).

The composer Shri Gūḷūra Siddhavīraṇārya states that the first compilation of Shunya Sampadane by Shivagaṇaprasādi Mahādevayya did not include the chapter on the process of initiation of Siddharamayya, but the later third compilation by Siddhaliṅgadēvaru of Gommaḷāpura had incorporated that chapter in it. Thus, adopting the contents and the method of Siddhaliṅgadēvaru, the composer Gūḷūra Siddhavīraṇārya has compiled his own version which is the fourth version of Shunya Sampadane.

Shunya Sampadane is the quintessence of the Veerashaiva Philosophy

Shunya Sampadane is the quintessence of the Veerashaiva Philosophy. It is composed mainly in the form of discourses among various Veerashaiva Sharanas. The central figure of Shunya Sampadane is Allama Prabhudeva. He presided over the deliberations in the Anubhava Mantapa the Academy of Sharanas.

The main theme of discussion at the Academy was the Shatsthala Philosophy. **Shatsthala** is the most important spiritual doctrine and religious practice of the Veerashaivas. Prabhudeva brought about a synthesis of various paths that lead to liberation/salvation. These deliberations have been incorporated in the Shunya Sampadane in the form of vachanas. Shunya Sampadane has twenty-one chapters.

In the concluding remarks given at the end of volume five of reference one, Shunya Sampadane gives this list of statements (1):

- This is the best guide, the philosophical system of exalted Veerashaiva doctrine.
- This is that which expounds and firmly establishes the Veerashaiva practice.
- This is the crest-jewel of the divine Vedanta.
- This is the chief mirror of all the sciences.
- This is the teaching of the highest Experience to promote the Supreme Knowledge.
- This is a catalogue of those who, endowed with all kinds of religious practice, have attained the Height.
- This is a treasury of the attainment of the great Raja Yoga.
- This is a happy feast of the ambrosial essence of Existence-Consciousness-Bliss, eternal and perfect.
- This is a great conference of Prabhudeva on the attainment of Shunya – an instrument to remove ignorance.

This concluding remark is a profound statement. It has a great impact on the philosophy and practice of the Veerashaivas. Although the vachana literature is the basic scripture, Shunya Sampadane is considered as the main scripture of the Veerashaivas because of the way the vachanas are composed in the form of discourses among various 12th century philosophers.

It is to be pointed out that the third one on the above list of the concluding remarks states **'This is the crest-jewel of the divine Vedanta'**. The term 'Vedanta' primarily refers to the Upanishads. The Shunya Sampadane and Upanishad connection is explained in the following article.

SHUNYA SAMPADANE AND THE UPANISHADS

The third one on the list of the nine statements of the concluding remarks in Shunya Sampadane (1) states: *'This is the crest-jewel of the divine Vedanta'.* The term *'Vedanta'* in that statement primarily refers to the Upanishads.

It is said that the Upanishads are the authorities for the formulation of the religious as well as the philosophical concepts of the Veerashaivas (6). The most important one of all the Veerashaiva concepts is the Shatsthala system. In this system, spiritual assent in six stages involves devotion, knowledge, and action. **Development of the Shatsthala system, by harmoniously combining true-devotion, knowledge, and action, has been through the influence of the Upanishads** (6).

The referenced Shunya Sampadane (1) which has five volumes, has lists of abbreviated references at the beginning of each of its five volumes. Many of these abbreviated references are for the Upanishads.

- Volume I has a list of 76 references, and 38 of them are for the Upanishads.
- Volume II has a list of 57 references, and 5 are for the Upanishads.
- Volume III has a list of 79 references, and 9 are for Upanishads.

- Volume IV has a list of 59 references, and 4 are for Upanishads.
- Volume V has a list of 25 references, but there are no references to Upanishads.

More importantly, it is not just the number of references to the Upanishads, it is how the Upanishads are incorporated into the Veerashaiva scriptures that is brought out by the Shunya Sampadane. This 'List of Abbreviations' does not indicate how often each of the references is quoted or referred to.

In addition to the above references to the Upanishads, Shunya Sampadane editors refer to Rigveda, Bhagavad-Gita, and such scriptures. All these references and particularly the references to the Upanishads are repeatedly quoted and explained in the introduction section as well as in the notes section of Shunya Sampadane (1).

The vachanas are said to be comparable to the Upanishadic sayings of the great ancient sages (1). The vachanas are very inspirational and appealing to the people. They are full of spiritual insight and have mystic overtones. (1).

However, it seems that some Veerashaivas believe that the vachanas of Sharanas of the 12th century, condemn the Vedas entirely. But it is to be pointed out to the readers that this does not seem to be the case on the basis of what is in the vachanas themselves.

Vedas, in all, are generally considered to have two portions. The first part is the portion dealing with action or rituals (*karma kāṇḍa*) with the belief that salvation/liberation (*Moksha*) can be obtained through the right performance of rituals as enjoined by the Vedas. And the second part comes at the end of the Vedas, in the Upanishads, dealing with knowledge (*jñāna kāṇḍa*). This second part is said to be the quintessence of the Vedas.

When one scrutinizes the vachana literature, one will realize that the Sharanas do not condemn the Vedas in total and Upanishads in particular. Study of the vachanas reveals the following information:

- The Sharanas of the 12th century condemn the first ritualistic part of the Vedas that prescribe sacrificial ceremonies and such. This portion of the Vedas is mostly in the Brahmanas that are attached to the Vedas, and to some extent in the Samhitas of the Vedas. Samhita is the main portion of a Veda.
- The vachanas condemn the sacrificial ceremonies and other ritualistic practices propounded by the first part of the Vedas.
- They condemn the people who perform those sacrificial ceremonies and the ritualistic practices.
- They do not condemn the second part (*Jñāna-kāṇḍa*) of the Vedas which is mainly the

Upanishads. They seem to embrace this portion of the Vedas.

- Basavanna, Chennabasavanna, Prabhudeva and some of the other Sharanas were very well versed in the Vedas, and in general they do not condemn the Vedas entirely.
- They make it known that the study and the knowledge of the Vedas is not necessary to attain the Absolute (Shunya).

Therefore, it can be stated that Sharanas do not condemn the Vedas entirely. Through the influence of the Upanishads, the Sharanas have developed the Shatsthala system by harmoniously combining true-devotion, knowledge, and action.

Upanishads are the best known aspects of the Vedic literature. Upanishads contain the esoteric spiritual knowledge meant for reflection and contemplation. The Upanishads do not have a single author.

The Upanishads mention that the nature of the Reality is that it is Infinite where one sees nothing hears nothing and understands nothing; and that the Reality is transcendent meaning that it is indefinable, attribute-less and free from all relationship. The knowledge of Reality is the knowledge pertaining to one's own Self. It is through the Self-knowledge that one knows anything and everything.

Vachana literature is similar to that of the Upanishads. Both the vachanas and the

Upanishads do not have a single author; both have differing viewpoints; both contain the ultimate goal of realization; meditation on the Supreme Self as the way of redemption is the theme in both.

Both the Vachanas and the Upanishads teach the same thing: Nature of the Absolute Reality is that it is Infinite where one sees nothing hears nothing and understands nothing. Truth is open for thorough inquiry, and that, being universal, it can be realized in anyone's life at any time. It is not reserved for any one privileged person or a group, nor is it confined by time or space.

Thus, one cannot just dismiss the Vachanas and the Upanishads.

SHUNYA *(ŚŪNYA)*

The term 'Shunya' is applied here for the 'Absolute Reality'. The literal meaning of 'Shunya' is 'void' or 'emptiness' or 'nothing-ness'. It conveys the meaning that there is nothing, yet there is something. It is at once Naught and Aught, Non-being and Being. It is neither form nor formlessness, neither time nor timelessness. It is indivisible, without a second, existence-consciousness-bliss, eternal and perfect.

Shunya has no attributes and cannot be worshipped directly.

Prabhudeva describes Shunya in one of his vachanas (page ix in volume I of reference 1). It is as follows:

This is the true height of the nature of the undivided Absolute Divine:
It is neither form nor formlessness – this undivided Absolute;
It is neither time nor timelessness;
It is neither of this nor of the other world;
Not touched by sorrow or by joy;
Above all merit and all sin;
It is neither cause nor consequence;
Not bound by duty or by works;
Not worshipped nor the worshipper;
Thus, being beyond all sense of duality,
It shines – our Guheshvara-Linga!

The term 'Guheshvara-Linga' in the above vachana refers to the Absolute Divine. The above vachana is self-explanatory. But, please note that the Absolute has no attributes – no form, no qualities, nothing inside it, nothing attached to it, there is no outside – there is nothing. Furthermore, it is to be pointed out that this undivided Absolute cannot be worshipped directly.

'Pūrṇa' of the Upanishads describes Shunya of the Veerashaivas

In the Preface section of the referenced Shunya Sampadane (1), the editors of volume I of Shunya Sampadane, state that Shunya of the Veerashaiva Sharanas is identical with the Upanishadic word *'Pūrṇa'* found in the following peace-lesson *(śāntipāṭha)*, and then they give the transliterated version of the peace-lesson. But the English translation of this peace-invocation is not given there. It is not clear why they did not, but it is given here below.

All the Upanishads begin with one or more peace invocations before the main part of the teachings of the Upanishads starts. The Upanishads also end with the same or a different peace invocation.

Ishavasya Upanishad (7) has this peace invocation referred to above by the editors of volume I of Shunya Sampadane. It is at the beginning as well as at the end of Ishavasya Upanishad. Brihadaranyaka Upanishad (8) and

Shvetashvatara Upanishad (9) also use the same peace invocation.

The term *'Pūrṇa'* with a long vowel 'u' and a retroflex/cerebral consonant 'n' the sound of which is produced with the tongue bent backwards, comes seven times in this peace invocation.

'Oṁ pūrṇamadaḥ pūrṇamidaṁ
pūrṇāt pūrṇamudaĉyate
pūrṇasya pūrṇamādāya
pūrṇamevāvaśiṣyate.'
Oṁ! Śāntiḥ! Śāntiḥ! Śāntiḥ!

'Pūrṇa' is translated as *'infinite'* and also as *'whole'*. The words in parenthesis in the following peace invocation are not in the original invocation. But those words are included here to give the peace invocation its full meaning.

'Om, that (invisible) is the Infinite, this (visible) too is the Infinite; from the Infinite the whole (universe) has arisen. Of the Infinite the whole (universe) having come, the Infinite alone remains the same. Om! Peace! Peace! Peace!'

In the above translation, when 'Pūrṇa' is translated as 'Infinite', it refers to the 'Absolute'. And when 'Pūrṇa' is translated as 'whole' it refers to the universe. Even after the manifestation of the universe, the Absolute remains the same. Everything is only one and it is the Absolute. It is to this Absolute – the Infinite – that the Shunya Sampadane refers to as Pūrṇa. And it is the Shunya of the Veerashaivas.

The editors of Shunya Sampadane (1) further state that the word 'Shunya' of the Veerashaiva Sharanas indicates the Infinite, the Absolute, the Brahman or Parabrahman of the Upanishads. And that 'Shunya' of the Veerashaivas is not unreal as that of the Buddhists and it is not the Shunyata of the Madhyamika Buddhists.

The main aim of the Veerashaivas is the attainment of the Absolute – that is Shunya Sampadane. Some have translated 'Shunya Sampadane' to mean 'Acquisition of Nothing'.

The vachanas also use another term ***'Bayalu'*** to refer to the same 'Absolute' as that of 'Shunya'. Shunya and Bayalu are the two most common terms used in the vachanas for the Absolute Reality. Although the term 'Bayalu' conveys the same meaning – Void - as that of Shunya, its meaning is more akin to the term 'Infinite'.

It may be interesting to note the following:

- In Basavaṇṇa's vachanas, Shūnya comes about 12 times, and Bayala/Bayalu comes about 22 times.
- In Allama Prabhudēva's vachanas, Shūnya comes about 148 times, and Bayala/Bayalu comes about 88 times.
- In Chennabasavaṇṇa's vachanas, Shūnya comes about 50 times, and Bayala/Bayalu comes about 26 times.

Further, the following is to be noted:

- It is notable that the vachanas do not use the term 'Shiva' for the Absolute.
- The Absolute has no attributes – no qualities, nothing inside it, nothing attached to it, there is no outside – there is nothing.
- The Absolute cannot be worshipped directly.

THE DIVINITY

Oneness Philosophy of the Sharanas is Theistic Monism meaning that the Absolute Reality itself is God. Everything including the Self is God.

In the vachanas, each Sharana uses one's own signature title for this Absolute Divinity. For example, Allama Prabhudeva uses the vachana signature 'Guheshvara' and sometimes 'Guheshvara-Linga' for the Absolute Divinity. Similarly, Basavanna uses 'Kudala Sangama Deva', and Chennabasavanna uses 'Kudala Chenna-Sangama Deva' for the same Absolute Divinity.

In the vachanas, the Sharanas adore the Absolute Divinity. This adoration may give the impression that God and Sharana are separate entities. It is not the case. Everything is only one. It is the Advaita Philosophy.

Two vachana examples of adoration and also depiction of the Absolute Divinity are given below.

Allama Prabhudeva adores and also describes the Absolute Divinity being everywhere. Vachana 14 on pages 21 and 22 in volume V of Shunya Sampadane (1) is something like this:

Lord, you are found on mountains,
In caves and in vales,
Yet you do not touch the ground!

Lord, you are found wherever one looks!
Incomprehensible, invisible, you are
Here, there and everywhere!
O Guheshvara,
I have seen you wherever I have roamed!

Description of the Absolute Divinity being everywhere, as in the above vachana, is continued in the following vachana of Allama Prabhudeva. Vachana 25 on page 32 in volume V of Shunya Sampadane is as follows (1):

This world and the other world
Are where he is;
The sky and Meru's mansion
Are where he is;
All the worlds and the true spheres
Are where he is;
The pure, eternal principles are where he is;
The higher and the highest ranks
Are where he is;
The orbits of the sun, the moon
And the stares are where he is;
Space and the outer space are where he is;
The self-subsistent Guheshvara
Is where he is.

The Absolute Divinity is everywhere. It has in it everything including the whole universe.

The following vachanas that are in Shunya Sampadane, are examples where Allama

Prabhudeva is describing the Absolute Divinity to Siddharamayya (1).

In this following vachana, Allama Prabhudeva says that the Absolute Divinity cannot be grasped by simple flattery. Vachana 43 on pages 257 and 258 in volume I of Shunya Sampadane is as follows:

You cannot grasp Him, as you can
Those who have donned the body.
He does not move this way and that,
As breathing mortals do.
You cannot size Him up with eyes,
Nor measure Him with ears.
Look you, O Siddharamayya
Guheshvara's glory
Cannot be grasped by simple flattery!

The same theme continues in the next vachana of Allama Prabhudeva. One cannot catch the Absolute Divinity by the words of flattery. Vachana 44 on pages 258 and 259 in volume I of Shunya Sampadane is something like this:

Though you can see Him,
He has no form;
Though you can seize Him
He has no body.
Although He moves He has no motion;
Although He speaks, He has no speech.
To those who curse Him, He is not a foe;
To those who praise Him, He is not a friend.

If you hope to catch
Guheshvara's glory in a net of words,
You must be a fool O Siddharamayya!

Allama Prabhudeva, continuing his teaching, states that the Sense-transcending Absolute Divinity lies beyond the enlightened face. Vachana 52 on page 267 in volume I of Shunya Sampadane is as follows:

You cannot catch Him, though you wish
To clasp Him with your body.
You cannot clasp Him, though you wish
To clasp Him with your breath.
You cannot catch Him, though you wish
To clasp Him with your heart.
You cannot catch Him, though you wish
To clasp Him where the subtle body's mind
Sharpens to a peak.
Look, the disembodied one,
Sense-transcending Absolute lies beyond
The farthest reach of the
Enlightened countenance!
Tell me Siddharamayya, by what means
You stay Guheshvara's devotee?

In the next vachana Allama Prabhudeva says that the Divinity is beyond words and beyond imagination, and that one cannot describe or imagine what the Divinity is. Vachana 101 on pages 316 and 317 in volume I of Shunya Sampadane is as follows:

How ineffable the un-manifest Supreme?

How manifest the ineffable Supreme?
It is not as simple as an idle talk!
Look you, Guheshvara-Linga
Is not imagination's toy!

In yet another vachana, Allama Prabhudeva, says that The Absolute Divinity cannot be known through any type of empirical knowledge. Vachana 103 on pages 318 and 319 in volume I of Shunya Sampadane is as translated there (1):

You cannot go to school for Him;
He is not the ear's delight.
You cannot con Him from your holy books,
Nor glean Him from
The converse of the world.
He is not inward sense, nor outward form.
Unless you have the key to it,
What is the use of all you know?
Look you, O Siddharamayya,
Peerless is Guheshvara-Linga!

The above statement - one cannot know the Absolute Divinity by going to school and trying to learn about it, one cannot learn from reading the sacred scriptures, and that one cannot know the Absolute Divinity by any other type of empirical knowledge - is a profound statement. This concept is in Katha Upanishad (10). Katha Upanishad is one of the major Upanishads.

The statement is the first half of the passage I.II.23 which is also referred to as passage II.23, in the Katha Upanishad. It is as follows (10):

'This Ātman cannot be attained by the study of the Vedas, nor by intellect, nor even by much learning.'

It is interesting to note that the Sanskrit compound word *'pravachanena'* in the above Katha Upanishad passage has been translated as 'by the study of the Vedas'. This Sanskrit compound word does not contain the term 'Veda' in it, but it contains the word 'vachana'. Here 'vachana' has been translated as 'Veda'. Vachana apparently means the sacred saying in Sanskrit.

LINGA *(LIṄGA)*

Shūnya, the Absolute Reality, has no attributes and cannot be worshipped directly. Therefore, Veerashaivas have conveniently adopted 'Liṅga' as the highest principle that could be worshipped.

The striking thing in the vachanas, as compared to the Sanskrit scriptures namely Shivagamas and Siddhanta Shikhamani, is that the emphasis is on Linga here in Shunya Sampadane, not on Shiva.

This emphasis on Liṅga becomes evident as one reads the Shūnya Sampādane text. However, in order to show this in a simple way (not as proof) is to see how often the terms 'Liṅga' and 'Shiva' come in the referenced Shūnya Sampādane (1), and the vachanas themselves (3).

- In the referenced Shunya Sampadane (1), on the basis of the index at the end of the five volumes, Linga comes there about 584 times, and Shiva comes there about 115 times. This index refers to the text of introduction and comments as well as to the vachanas.

In the Ganaka Vachana Samputa reference (3) which has all the vachanas, the incidence of appearance of the two words is as follows:

- In 1426 vachanas of Basavanna, Linga comes 559 times, and Shiva comes 203 times.

- In 1645 vachanas of Allama Prabhudeva, Linga comes 1,391 times, and Shiva comes 226 times.
- In 1791 vachanas of Chennabasavanna, Linga comes 2,112 times, and Shiva comes 534 times.
- In 354 vachanas of Akka Mahadevi, Linga comes 144 times, and Shiva comes 51 times in 34 vachanas.
- In 1679 vachanas of Siddharamayya, Linga comes 591 times, and Shiva comes 219 times.
- It seems to be the same in the vachanas of other Sharanas.

Linga and its coming to the palm

The following vachana describes the Linga and its coming to the palm.

Allama Prabhudeva's vachana 53 on pages 101 and 102 in volume I of Shunya Sampadane is like this (1):

When the invisible Linga
Has come to my palm, what can I say?
To me this is wonder of wonders!
The Guheshvara-Linga,
Without form, without bound,
Has taken form and has come to my palm.
How can I speak?

The invisible Linga has come to the palm. The Absolute Divine which has no form and has no bounds has taken form and has come to the palm as Linga. Allama Prabhudeva says he is speechless because of this Linga coming to the palm.

Please note that Allama Prabhudeva does not use the term Ishtalinga in the above vachana. The Absolute Linga comes to the palm as Linga. Therefore, the Linga on the palm is the same as the Absolute Linga. One should not try to differentiate the two.

Ishtalinga ***(Iṣṭaliṅga)*** is the physical form of Linga that is worn on the body throughout one's life, and when the person dies, it is buried in the ground with the dead body. Unlike most Hindus who cremate the dead body on a pyre, Veerashaivas bury the dead body.

Ishtalinga is the symbolic Linga used for worshipping and longing for the attainment of the true Linga.

Karasthala: Kara-sthala is the place on the palm of the hand where the Ishtalinga is held, and where the Ishtalinga is worshipped. In the sitting position, Ishtalinga is held on the palm of the outstretched left hand at the level of one's heart. While worshipping, the external world is ignored and the eyes are focused on the Ishtalinga/Karasthala.

Sthala simply means that it is a place or a station. But it is said that the highest application of the term 'Sthala' is for Supreme-Brahman which has been called Sthala, Brahman, Ātman, and Linga. The Supreme-Ātma-Linga is the resort and the cause of the Universe. Sthala in a way is this resort. **Karasthala is considered not different from the Supreme-Ātma-Linga-Sthala.** It is an important concept of the Veerashaivas.

The main part of Ishtalinga worship is gazing upon the Linga on the palm. One needs to focus on it and contemplate.

Ishtalinga is worshipped privately by the individuals. The worship is not done in public, and definitely not done for applause or admiration. To an ordinary devotee, the Ishtalinga worship is helpful to strengthen the will. First there is worship of the Ishtalinga. Then the worship shifts to the internal worship of the formless internal Linga.

It is said that the obedient worship of Ishtalinga by a disciple as advised by the Guru, takes the disciple to heaven as a reward. Going to heaven does not result in liberation from the cycle of births and deaths, and does not result in the attainment of oneness with Linga. Once the devotee strengthens one's own will, one should change to worshipping internal Linga in order to advance spiritually.

Undue preoccupation with traditional or customary rites and rituals associated with the Ishtalinga worship are condemned by Allama Prabhudeva (1). He says something like this in the two vachanas on pages 23 and 24 in volume I of Shunya Sampadane (1):

If one ties a packet of food to the belly, would the hunger go away?

If one hangs fast an Ishtalinga to one's trunk, would one become a bhakta?

If one fixes a stone on a bush, is that stone a Linga?

Will that bush become a bhakta? And is the one who put it there a Guru?

When I see such a one, O Guheshvara, I blush for shame.

I blush to see those who pluck the outer Ishtalinga and worship the outer...

But if I see a wink-less Linga within and worship it within the flower of my mind,

The shame ebbs, and I am all free from doubt, O Guheshvara!

Ishtalinga worship can be summarized as follows:

- Ishtalinga is the physical form of Linga that is worn on the body.
- Ishtalinga is the symbolic Linga used for worshipping and longing for the attainment of the true Linga.
- For worshipping purposes, Ishtalinga is held on the palm of the outstretched left hand at the level of one's heart, and the eyes are focused on the Ishtalinga.
- Ishtalinga is worshipped privately by the individuals. The worship is not done in public, and definitely not done for applause or admiration.

- The real worship is not with material things. It is with pure devotion and knowledge.
- First there is worship of the Ishtalinga. Then the worship shifts to the internal worship of the formless internal Linga.
- Individuals are responsible for working out their own relation to Linga.

The question whether every Sharana must wear Ishtalinga on one's body comes up when Prabhudeva brings the great Shivayogi Siddharamayya to the Academy of Sharanas (Anubhava Mantapa) at Kalyana. Shivayogi Siddharamayya was not wearing Ishtalinga on his body because he had not been invested with one before. This has been discussed very well in chapter ten that is to come later on in this book.

Shūnya Saṁpādane

Shūnya Saṁpādane is briefly described here in this book. The information is from the fourth version of Shūnya Sampādane compiled in the later part of the sixteenth century by Gūḷūra Siddhavīraṇārya. It is as given in ŚŪNYASAṀPĀDANE published by the Karnāṭaka University, Dharwad, India. (1).

This Shūnya Sampādane has twenty-one chapters.

Chapter 1

PRABHUDĒVA'S SHŪNYA SAMPĀDANE

The first of the twenty-one chapters begins with three stanzas of obeisance. In the first stanza, the obeisance is to Siddhaliṅgasudēshika, and in the second it is for Bōḷabasavēshārya, both are said to be the author's teachers. In the third stanza, the author Gūḷūra Siddhavīraṇārya introduces himself, states that it is a record of Prabhudēva's teaching, and dedicates it to him.

After the dedication in the stanzas, in the prose section of Shūnya Saṁpādane, Gūḷūra Siddhavīraṇārya briefly describes the Veerashaiva concept of the Creation. It is not just the creation aspect, it is also the regaining of identity with the Absolute in reverse of the creation. It is as follows:

The Creation

Nishkala Linga is the Absolute Linga.

'In the beginning the Undivided Linga (*Nishkala Linga*), indivisible, without a second, peerless, without parts, spotless, inclusive of the entire Void, which is existence, knowledge, bliss, eternity and perfection - in order not to remain as Void, by an impulse of spontaneous play and sport, putting forth the glow of Consciousness, created within Self, an infinity of macrocosms *(Brahmāṇḍa)* and myriad of microcosms *(Ātma)*.

'And when the twenty-five categories (*tattvas*) were attached to the souls *(Ātma)*, the souls forgot their true nature, and in asserting their body, became subject to caste and sect and stages of life (*varṇāshramadharma*), to pleasure and pain, to freedom and bondage, and became captive to desire and death. They became subject to the worldly life cycle of births and deaths (*samsāra*).

'But some of them receiving the touch of the Spirit in the form of Guru, Linga and Jangama, learnt to despise the influence of corporeal existence and achieved freedom from the worldly life of births and deaths. The same Spirit (*Nishkala-Para-Shiva-Linga*) bestowing grace upon them, made them one with its own Supreme-Self.'

The above concept of the creation can be explained in a summary form as follows:

- The Integral Absolute is only one.
- The Absolute Linga putting forth the glow of Consciousness creates within Self an infinity of macrocosms and myriad of microcosms (souls).
- Ātma (soul) is the manifestation of the Divine Will, and it is within Linga itself.
- It is the spontaneous sport or play that is actuated in the Absolute for the manifestation of Linga out of compassion for the souls as the true-devotees who would worship Linga.
- Then the attachment of 25 principles to the souls resulted in the physical body being attached to the souls and the creation of the material world/universe.
- When the twenty-five categories get attached to the souls, the souls forget their true nature and become captive to desire and death. They become subject to the worldly life cycle of births and deaths.
- The souls receiving the touch of grace in the form of Guru, Linga and Jangama, learn to despise the influence of corporeal existence and achieve freedom from the worldly life of births and deaths.
- The bestowal of grace upon them makes them to become one with the Absolute Linga.

The above description is in the prose section of Shunya Sampadane as narrated by the composer. Additional information about creation is in the vachanas themselves, particularly in the vachanas of the Piṇḍa-jñāna-sthala (given later in this book).

Part of the above description of creation states: 'And when the twenty-five categories (*tattvas*) were attached to the souls *(Ātma)*...' It is to be pointed out that the twenty-five categories (tattvas) mentioned here are as described in the Sāṁkhya Philosophical system. The Shaivas and the Veerashaivas believe that there are thirty-six tattvas, eleven more coming before the other twenty-five tattvas. Reason for this disparity is not clear. These tattvas represent the modification of Parashivabrahman, resulting in the creation of this universe. More information is in the book 'Veerashaivism' (reference 2).

Further, it is to be pointed out that there is no 'Vimarsha-shakti' in any of the vachanas. Therefore it is not involved in any way in this concept of creation.

The dictionary meaning of 'vimarsha' is 'Self-conscious, universal consciousness, knowledge, intelligence, consideration, power of discrimination, power to judge, and such. The term 'vimarsha' is an explanatory noun; it is not a proper noun. It is not a separate entity.

Some of the comments by the editors of volume I of Shunya Sampadane are notable:

All the Veerashaiva Philosophers hold that the world is evolved out of nothing. In the beginning there was nothing, not even Shunya or

Nisshunya. Then Sharana arose. This is the fundamental theory of Veerashaiva Sharanas. Then the editors state that in the Rigveda hymn of creation, the same idea is found.

The editors quote the verse X.129.1 from Nāsadīya-sukta of Rigveda (11, 12). Na-sad means non-existent. It is as follows:

'nāsadāsīnno sadāsīttadānīṁ nāsīdrajo no vyomā para yat'

There was not the non-existent nor the existent then; there was not the air nor the heaven which is beyond.

In addition the editors state that in Chandogya Upanishad VI.2.1 it is stated that there was a school of philosophers who held that *'asat'* (non-existence) was in the beginning, and from *'asat' 'sat'* (existence) issued (13).

Introduction of Prabhudeva

After the description of Creation, the author Gūḷūra Siddhavīraṇārya introduces Prabhudeva. Some of the introductory remarks concerning Prabhudeva are as follows:

Illumined with Great Knowledge; the Lord of the eightfold yoga – *yama, niyama, asana, pranayama, pratyahara, dhyana, dharana and samadhi* (please note that the order of dhyāna and dhāraṇa has been reversed in the text of reference 1) - untainted, perfect embodiment of eternity, embraced and anointed with the Linga; the teacher who established Guru, Linga, Jangama, Prasada, Padodaka, etc.; the sovereign of the six-fold hierarchy Shatsthala - Bhaktasthala, Maheshvarasthala, Prasadisthala, Pranalingisthala, Sharanasthala and Aikyasthala; the crest jewel of glorious Veerashaiva faith; the prime leader of the glorious Veerashaiva faith; the preceptor who confers initiation of the glorious Veerashaiva faith; the great teacher who conducted high discourses on Shunya Sampadane with innumerable great devotees; and many such glorifications.

It is to be pointed out to the readers that Prabhudeva is introduced above as the lord of the eight-fold yoga, and then the eight stages of the yoga are given. This eight-fold yoga is Patañjali's Ashṭāṅga Yoga. It is also called Raja Yoga. Further, it is to be pointed out that in the concluding remarks of Shunya Sampadane, the seventh of the nine statements in the list is *'This is a treasury of the attainment of the great Raja Yoga'*. Therefore, it seems that the Shatsthala is not only influenced by the Upanishads, but also based on the Raja Yoga.

The first three introductory articles in the referenced Shunya Sampadane (1) are about Allama Prabhudeva. The editors give the following information in these articles:

Prabhudeva lived in the 12th century of the Common Era (CE). He was born at Balligavi, a village in the Shivamogga District of Karnataka

State, India. His father's name is said to be Nirahankara, and that of his mother Sujnana.

Nothing is known about Prabhudeva's upbringing. But he was very well versed in the Vedas and other sacred Hindu scriptures. He had apparently gone through all kinds of Yoga, particularly the eight-fold Raja Yoga. It is said that he had travelled across the length and breadth of India as a vagrant ascetic, had met hundreds of seekers, and had several types of experiences, prior to the Supreme Experience through the great Animisha, his Guru. Prabhudeva's encounter with the great Guru Animisha is recorded in this first chapter of Shunya Sampadane under Lingadhāraṇa-sthala.

Prabhudeva, through Yoga, had realized what is known as *'Bayalu dēha'* or *Shunya kāya*, which may be rendered as *'ethereal body'* or *'glorified body'*. In this defiled state he was able to perform miracles/wonders.

His main concern was to lead other seekers to the same spiritual perfection, by revealing to them the meaning of Shunya. Prabhudeva was the 'moving spirit' of Shunya Sampadane. He moved from place to place, to wherever he knew there was a seeker who needed aid, and helped him or her realize oneself.

Prabhudeva is the central character in Shunya Sampadane. The Shunya Sampadane contains the quintessence of Prabhudeva's achievement and teaching. It can be said that the whole of Shunya Sampadane is the detailed description of the Jangama nature of Prabhudeva.

Prabhudeva was the ideal Jangama, and everything in Shunya Sampadane is about this Supreme Jangama.

SHATSTHALA *(ṢAṬSTHALA)*

The compiler of the fourth version of Shunya Sampadane Gūḷūra Siddhavīraṇārya, in this first chapter, presents 78 Prabhudeva's Shatsthala vachanas. The following part of the first chapter containing the Shatsthala vachanas is the most important part of Shunya Sampadane.

The Veerashaiva concept of Shatsthala is the spiritual hierarchy of six stages through which the seeker rises stage by stage till the apparent duality vanishes and attainment of oneness occurs. This process of attaining oneness, becoming Shunya itself, is called Shunya Sampadane.

The Shaṭsthalas are Bhaktasthala, Maheshvarasthala, Prasadisthala, Pranalingisthala, Sharanasthala and Aikyasthala.

In the prose section of Shunya Sampadane, there is a brief statement about Shatsthala. It is as follows:

- When the faith in the Ishtalinga obtained through the Guru's grace grows, the Ishtalinga becomes Āyatalinga. 'Āyata' means 'what is come'.
- When the spirit of that Ishtalinga penetrates the heart, the Pranalinga becomes Svāyataliṅga. 'Svayata' means 'what is made one's own'.
- When the spirit of Ishtalinga and the joy that has penetrated the mind appears the same,

and completely fills with ineffable peace, the Bhāvaliṅga becomes Sannahitaliṅga. 'Sannahita' means 'what inhabits one'.

- When Ishtalinga Pranalinga and Bhāvaliṅga have become Āyatalinga Svāyataliṅga and Sannahitaliṅga in the triple body, the six kinds of Linga join together with the six Angas of the Sharana, and then that is Shatsthala.

The above statement in the prose section is in the vachanas of Allama Prabhudēva. Two of those vachanas are in Shūnya Sampādane itself. One of these is vachana 138 on pages 356 and 357 in volume I of Shūnya Saṁpādane (1). Allama Prabhudēva is advising Siddharāmayya in that vachana. The other is vachana 82 on page 203 in volume II of Shūnya Saṁpādane (1). Allama Prabhudēva is praising Basavaṇṇa in this vachana. The second vachana is as follows:

I found my ancient teacher
In what is 'Come' (Āyata).
I found my ancient teacher
In what is 'Made One's Own' (Svāyata).
I found my ancient teacher
In what 'Inhabits One' (Sannahita).
Hail! O hail to Thy holy feet,
My ancient teacher Saṅgana Basavaṇṇa
Abiding in Guheshvara-Liṅga!

***'What is come'* is Linga, *'what is made one's own'* is Linga, and *'what inhabits one'* is Linga.**

The six **Aṅga** parts are not mentioned in the main part of Shunya Sampadane, but they are given in the introductory part as well as in the notes and comments section. Six Angas are said to be the five sense organs and the mind – nose sensing smell, tongue sensing taste, eye sensing sight, skin sensing touch, ear sensing hearing, and the heart where mind is said to be located.

Shatsthala, as has been pointed out before, not only is influenced by the Upanishads, but also is based on the Raja Yoga. **The Yoga of the Veerashaivas is based on the Upanishads and the Raja Yoga.**

Piṇḍasthala

Shunya Sampadane begins with Piṇḍasthala. The Piṇḍasthala is one of the preliminary steps to Bhaktasthala. In Piṇḍasthala, piṇḍa means a purified individual-self aspiring to be united with the Universal-Self. In spiritual terms, the soul is still in the stage of a fetus.

The characteristic of this step is that the aspiring person visualizes the existence of Linga in one's own body.

This Divine immanence can be recognized only by one who is aspiring to achieve the goal.

In Shunya Sampadane, only two vachanas are given in this preliminary sthala.

The first vachana of Allama Prabhudeva in Shunya Sampadane explains the nature of Divine immanence by means of similes:

As a spark in stone,
As an image in water,
As a tree in the seed,
As silence in speech,
So Thou in Thy devotee
O Guheshvara.

In the second vachana Allama Prabhudeva says that Linga cannot be perceived by a common person, but the one who experiences the joy of that realization knows it.

Can the spark in the stone kindle?
Can the tree in the seed rustle?
Guheshvara's majesty being unapparent,
Does not shine out for the common eye;
He only knows it
Who has tasted the joy of The Experience!

Prabhudēva makes an important point in his second vachana given above – ***this Divine Immanence does not show itself to a common person; the person has to want to know it and experience it.***

Although the editors of the referenced Shūnya Saṁpādane (1) have not indicated the following, it may be interesting to the readers to know that the concept of Divine Immanence in the vachanas is the same as that in the Upanishads. (14).

Shvetāshvatara-Upanishad (9) passage I.15 and Brahmopanishad (15) passage 19 have the same mantra quoted in the Shūnya Saṁpādane:

'As oil in sesame seeds, as butter in curds, as water in the underground springs, and as fire in wood, in like manner, this Ātman is perceived in the self by those who by means of truthfulness, self-control and concentration look again and again'.

Katha Upanishad (10) passage III.12 says: *'The Ātman hidden in all beings, reveals not, but is seen by seers of the subtle through focused and subtle intellect'.*

Aspiring person visualizes the existence of Linga in one's own body.

This Divine immanence can be recognized only by one who is aspiring to achieve the goal of realization.

Once the aspiring person visualizes the Divine immanence in one's own body, the person takes the next step given below - the person grasps the discriminative knowledge.

Piṇḍa-jñāna-sthala

In Piṇḍa-jnana-sthala, one grasps the discriminative knowledge and realizes that **the Ātman (the individual-Self) is totally different from the body, senses and the intellect.**

This concept that the soul is totally different from the body, senses, and intellect, is taken from many Upanishads. Kena Upanishad (16) passage I.2 says:

'It is the Ātman by whose power the ear hears, the eye sees, the tongue speaks, the mind understands, and life functions. The wise separate the Ātman from these faculties, rise out of sense-life, and attain immortality.'

Shunya Sampadane gives four vachanas for this preliminary sthala. In order to explain the eternal being who resides in the body, Allama Prabhudeva has this vachana about the Ātman. Vachana 3 on pages 57 and 58 of volume I of reference 1 is as follows:

When neither Source nor Substance was,
When neither I nor mine,
When neither Form nor Formless was,
When neither Void was nor non-Void,
Nor that which moves or moves not,
Then was Guheshvara's Sharana born.

Here, the term 'Sharana' has been used to mean Eternal Being, Consciousness or Ātman.

This 'Sharana' was there before the manifestation of Linga; there was no physical body or matter of any kind; the world/universe had not been created; and the Sharana was in a state of Pure Knowledge. Sharana is eternal and timeless.

It is important to understand that the **Ātman can be neither created nor destroyed**. The Integral Absolute is only one.

Then in the fourth vachana in Shunya Sampadane, five features of 'Sharana' are given. The term ***'Gaṇēshvara'*** is used here for the term Sharaṇa. Gaṇēshvara means the one who has attained and realized the Supreme. The five features are:

- The Sharana was **fearless** because there was no Nada, Bindu or Kala, and therefore was unattached to these or any other. [Nada, Bindu and Kala are said to originate at the time of creation.]
- The Sharana was **indestructible** because there was no birth, life or death.
- The Sharana was **Om-form** because there was neither learning nor knowing.
- The Sharana **existed before time** when there were neither eons nor ages.
- And Sharana was **without Māyā** (pronounced as Maayaa) in a state of Pure Knowledge before the distinction of Linga and Anga.

The fifth vachana in Shūnya Saṁpādane emphasizes the influence of Māyā. It is said that while Brahma, Vishṇu, Rudra, and multitude of Rishis were under the influence of Māyā and could not escape Māyā's firm grip, Prabhudēva vanquished Māyā.

Māyā is that which obstructs the understanding of Reality. It masks or hides the true identity, and thus results in ignorance and egoism. Under the duress of ignorance, it brings agony to everyone. More information about Māyā comes in the Māyāvilāsaviḍambana-sthala below.

Then, Allama Prabhudēva in this sixth vachana declares himself that for Bhakti's sake he appeared on earth during the four successive yugas:

In the Kritayuga, for bhakti's sake,
I appeared as Sthūlakāya Gaṇēshvara.
In the Trētāyuga, for bhakti's sake,
I appeared as Shūnyakāya Gaṇēshvara.
In the Dvāparayuga, for bhakti's sake,
I appeared as Animisha Gaṇēshvara.
In the Kaliyuga, for bhakti's sake,
I now appear as Allamaprabhu Gaṇēshvara,
O Guhēshvara.

The term *'Gaṇēshvara'* in the above vachana means the one who has attained and realized the Supreme. The terms *'Sthūla-kāya'* means gross-body, and *'Shūnya-kāya'* means ethereal-body or glorified-body. Animisha is Prabhudēva's Guru.

Yuga is an eon or ages. There are four yugas which come in cycles. The first one is the *Krita-yuga* also known as Satya-yuga, followed by *Trētā-yuga, Dvāpara-yuga,* and *Kali-yuga.* (2).

The present Yuga is the Kali-yuga. The Hindu traditionalists believe that Kali-yuga started after the disappearance of Divine Krishna and the submersion of Dvāraka Island in the Arabian Sea in the year 3,102 BCE. (2).

It is said that the explanation of the yugas involves a description of periods of time which belong to a scheme of chronology that is wholly mythological and not to any real history of the Hindus. (2).

Saṁsāraheyasthala

Saṁsāra is the cosmic process where one passes through a succession of births and deaths without any progress in breaking the cycle of births and deaths.

In Saṁsāraheyasthala one develops disgust for the worldly life of cycle of births and deaths, and detaches from the transient worldly pleasures by virtue of refined impressions.

There are ten vachanas in this preliminary sthala in Shunya Sampadane. The main point of teaching in the ten vachanas is that one has to break this cycle and attain immortality. The vachanas teach how to detach from these transient worldly pleasures and passions, and advance further in one's spiritual attainment.

Although in Piṇḍa-jñāna-sthala one has already grasped the discriminative knowledge that the Ātman (The Self) is totally different from the body, senses and the intellect, the soul not knowing its true nature identifies with the body. As a consequence the individual becomes fond of pleasures and passions associated with the body, and thus the individual is not in a position to realize the Divine presence.

Allama Prabhudeva's vachana - vachana 7 on pages 61 and 62 of volume I of Shunya Sampadane (1) is something like this:

The whole world knows not what seed
Was there before the body was;
The senses are not the seed,
Nay, not the elements one by one.
Delusions of dream have swooped upon us.
Verily, because no one understands,
There is no real peace, O Guheshvara.

All beings are subject to happiness and misery of worldly existence. A common person believes that the birth is the beginning and the death is the end and that that is all there is to life. The human beings with perishable bodies harbor instinctive cravings; and those who are caught in the cravings cannot realize the Divine. The individual is driven by a compelling passion for worldly pleasures. This thirst is not satisfied by enjoyment. The more one tries to appease the sense organs and the senses, the more dissatisfied one becomes. This causes distress and misery. Such an individual, fond of the body and pleasures associated with it, is not in a position to realize the Divine presence.

The individual has to understand that the body and the soul are not identical. One has to get rid of all the desires and passions such as lust, anger/aggression, greed, infatuation, boasting/ego and jealousy. There is no room for hatred or violence of any kind. These concepts are in many Upanishads (14).

One who has purged all desires and passions, attained contentment, and has

realized the difference between the body and the soul advances further in one's path towards the absolute.

Māyāvilāsaviḍambana-sthala

In Māyāvilāsaviḍambana-sthala the individual-self gets rid of Maya by recognizing that the Self is different from Maya and that the play of Maya is working against the realization of the Self.

The individual-self recognizes its identity to be one and the same as that of the Universal-Self.

In order to achieve this, one has to have a pure mind which is devoid of any restless activity, and has to have a clear consciousness. Stabilization of the mind is of prime importance so that one can then proceed on to contemplation and meditation in one's spiritual progress.

In Shunya Sampadane there are twelve vachanas that teach this sthala. These vachanas seem to be more enigmatic than many other enigmatic vachanas of Prabhudeva.

There is this complex vachana which needs a different explanation than the explanation given in the referenced Shūnya Saṁpādane. This complex vachana number 19 is on page 70 in volume I of Shūnya Saṁpādane (1). It is as follows:

On the tip of a horn of a male buffalo
There are 770 wells;
Each well contains a spring;
In that spring there is a harlot;

Around the neck of that harlot
I see 770 elephants crawling.
O Guheshvara!

The editors of volume I of the referenced Shunya Sampadane (1) explain the vachana on pages 378 and 379. The names of the editors of volume I are different from those of the other volumes as given in the article 'Shūnya Sampādane Texts' in this book. Some parts of this explanation are not correct and are not acceptable. The discussion is as follows:

The first part of the explanation is acceptable: The buffalo is the embodied individual-self Jiva (Jiva is soul). The Jiva, by its attachment to the body has fostered a false sense of agency which makes it a prey to pride. By coming into close contact with the sense objects it revels in sense of enjoyment. The 770 wells refer to 770 'nerves' in the body. Although the editors use the term 'nerve', they mean it to be 'nāḍi' which is sometimes referred to as 'nāḷa' in Kannada. Nāḍi or nāḷa is a pathway/conduit/channel through which the life-energy Prana courses through.

So far so good, but the disagreement starts after that:

- This disagreement is a minor point: The statement that 'the nerves are situated in the brain and spinal cord' is not correct. The nerves come out of the brain and spinal cord. The extensions of nerves into the brain and spinal cord are not called nerves.

- The statement that 'the spinal cord tapers into the coccyx' is not correct. The coccyx is nothing to do with the spinal cord. Coccyx is the lower end of the spine which is the backbone. The spinal cord which is part of the nervous system, ends higher up in the spinal canal in the lumbar-spine. The spinal canal is a hollow tube formed by the vertebrae stacked one on top of the other. Below the lumbar-spine there is the sacrum and below that is the coccyx.
- The editors imply that the coccyx is the Mūlādhāra Chakra. That is not correct. The Mūlādhāra chakra belongs to the Tantra system which is not applicable to the Veerashaivas. Further, coccyx is not the chakra, it is a bone; the Mūlādhāra chakra is located low down inside the body at the level of the coccyx.
- The editors state that the harlot in the vachana refers to Kundalini. This is really wrong. The harlot is Māyā, not Kundalini. Again Kuṇḍalini belongs to the Tantra system which is not applicable to the Veerashaivas. Further, Kundalini is not in any nāḍis. It stays dormant (coiled up) in Mūlādhāra Chakra. It has to be activated during Kundalini Yoga. When activated it goes up only in the central Sushumna nāḍi, not in any of those 770 nāḍis.
- The statement that 'Kundalini is named after her two coils - the Ida and Piṅgala' is definitely not correct. Kundalini is a form of energy that represents Shakti; it is nothing to do with these two nāḍis. Ida and Piṅgala are two spiral

nāḍis which spiral in a helical fashion around the central Sushumna nāḍi.

- The implication that this vachana describes the accessories of Kundalini Yoga is not acceptable at all; it is wrong. Veerashaivas do not practice the Tantra based Yogas.
- The editors have failed to recognize the Upanishad based concepts applicable to this vachana, and that this vachana comes under Māyāvilāsaviḍambana-sthala.
- The harlot in the 770 nāḍis is Maya influencing Prana, particularly the Prāṇa's sub-division Vyana which moves in all the nāḍis. The 770 elephants crawling around harlot's neck represent arrogance and insolence of Prana in the nāḍis that go in different directions. Maya influences the currents of life-force Prana. The Prana currents exist in the body in a haphazard manner and pose as obstacles for the orderly free flow of vital energy. One has to practice breath control (Upanishadic type of Pranayama, not the Tantra based one) in order to put these currants in a proper order of alignment. When poise/balance is established in the five divisions of Prana, the shackles of Maya are broken.

Further, the teaching in the vachanas is as follows:

The universe is a show. The phenomenal play within the universe is a show in a show. The work of the Creator disappears when real knowledge dawns. The phenomenal play within the universe is false; and when pure existence is realized, the phenomena disappear in to the deep-sleep. These three pertain to the three states of consciousness, namely, waking consciousness, dream consciousness and the deep-sleep consciousness. But the real Self-consciousness transcends these three states and abides in its native glory.

This state described in the vachana coincides with the description of ***'Turīya'***, the fourth state of consciousness. It is to be noted that although it is called the fourth state, it includes all the other three states. This consciousness is reflected in a pure mind which is devoid of restless activity. When pure mind and clear consciousness are identified, the silence reigns supreme. It is transcendental, devoid of all phenomenal existence, and it is ***'Shiva-advaita' the 'Supreme Bliss of Non-duality'***. All of this is the essence of the Mandukya Upanishad (14, 17). The actual term ***'Shiva-advaita'*** comes in the Mandukya Upanishad.

One who is caught up in the web of Maya continues to be ignorant without self-knowledge. So long as one regards the world to be distinct from the Self, the one is far from the Truth. One has to free oneself from the self-inflicted ignorance and acquire the right knowledge, and has to realize that the world is nothing but the manifestation of the Self. Then the phenomenal play ceases and the sense of duality is obliterated.

Under the influence of Maya, the ego flourishes; one displays an exaggerated sense of self-importance. In the path of spirituality, it is sheer ignorance to require commendation for performance; it is ego. The egotistic attitude has to be eliminated.

The soul, through ignorance, feeds upon the sense objects instead of extinguishing them. As a result the body becomes a vehicle of the three types of obstacles or sufferings - pertaining to mental and/or physical bodily afflictions; pertaining to sufferings from other terrestrial elements; and pertaining to celestial objects and such. When the body is burnt by the fire of triple pain, the Divine Self, being eternal, remains immune to such things.

Another vachana says as follows. The marvelous body is made of the combining together of five special elements – earth, water, fire, wind, and ether/sky/cosmos. When one forgets one's own real nature and identifies with the body, the fire of knowledge is extinguished, resulting in the mind enviously craving for possessions of others; the life, mind, and intellect remain impure and agitated so long as the stillness of the soul is not attained. The organ of mind is dominated by its object of desire, because one enviously desires what one does not have that others possess. This concept is in many Upanishads, but the referenced Brihadaranyaka Upanishad (8) passage III.2.7 is like this:

'The organ of mind is dominated by its object the desire, because one enviously desires what one does not have that others possess'.

The term 'monkey-mind' is used in the explanation of the restlessness of the mind. Just as a monkey jumps from branch to branch to pluck the fruit and eat it, the restless human mind leaps from one sense-organ to another to grasp at and enjoy the sense-objects. The restlessness of the mind is a huge hindrance in the way of discipline. Life, mind and intellect remain impure, if the stillness of the soul is not attained. Restless activities of the mind are to be brought to a stable status, not through force or suppression, but through persuasion, and by directing the expression towards a more socially or culturally acceptable way of life. Disciplining of the mind and the thought process is an important part for spiritual advancement; without that discipline, one cannot proceed to meditation.

One must not venture into any bad thoughts or thinking of harming other beings; at the verge of such, those thoughts are to be diverted into good thoughts or thoughts of helping others. Sometimes it may be necessary to avert such bad thoughts by chanting as many times as necessary, either silently or aloud, the simple mantra **'Om'**. Some may prefer to chant 'Om namaḥ Shivaya'. Some others may want to recite a vachana. Once the restlessness of the mind disappears, the mind itself merges with the Self.

The concept of Māyā in the vachanas can be summarized as follows:

- Maya plays tricks on one's mind so as to speak, and makes one's mind wander.
- Maya is that which obstructs one's understanding. It hides the true identity of oneness, and makes it appear as if it is two separate entities.
- The play of Maya works against the realization of the Self.
- Under the influence of Maya, the ego flourishes, and one displays an exaggerated sense of self-importance.
- Under the influence of Maya, one continues to be ignorant without self-knowledge, and regards the world to be distinct from one's own self.
- One has to free oneself from the self-inflicted ignorance and acquire the right knowledge. The individual-self has to rid itself of Maya by recognizing that the play of Maya is working against the realization of the Self.
- In order to achieve this, one has to have a pure mind which is devoid of any restless activity, and has to have a clear consciousness.
- As one realizes one's true nature and hence one's real identity, one discards the false glamour of the phenomenal world, and frees one's Self from the sinister influence of Maya.
- Maya is not Kundalini (not Shakti either).
- Maya does not create the universe.

Then there is this vachana, the twenty-ninth vachana, in which Prabhudeva upon encountering Gaggayya who was tilling his garden, suggests to him that he should also cultivate the Supreme as another garden. In this context Prabhudeva explains the whole process of self-realization. Using metaphor, he describes the process as follows:

- He states that he has made his body a garden.
- Using his mind as a spade, he has dug up the illusion's weeds – rooted out delusion; has broken up the clods of worldly-life; has cultivated the earth and sown Spirit's seed.
- His thousand-petal-lotus (Sahasrāra) located at the top of the brain, is his well, and his breath is his water-wheel.
- He channels water through the central channel (Sushumnā nāḍi) to irrigate the garden.
- To keep out the five bulls of senses, so as to prevent them trampling the crops, he sets up all around the garden, patience and poise as a fence.
- And he has lain awake night and day to protect his tender plants.

This intense vachana makes several points:

- The body is to be emptied out of its earthliness.
- The discriminating power of the mind is to be used to root-out the delusions.
- Breath-control is to be practiced to nurture spirituality and devotion.

- All sensory input is to be disengaged by using patience and poise in order to stabilize the mind so that the mind can be directed to carry out the function of contemplation and meditation.

Liṅgadhāraṇasthala

Liṅgadhāraṇa is the investiture of Linga by a Guru to a disciple. The prose sections and the vachanas 30 through 55 in Shunya Sampadane describe this sthala.

First is the aspect of the Guru. In the prose section, it is said that Prabhudeva through his own insight comes upon the trance-chamber of Animisha who is respectfully addressed as Animishadēva. And upon entering the chamber, finds Animishadēva in trance in the lotus position with his un-winking eyes focused on the Ishtalinga on his palm. At that instant, Prabhudeva was convinced that Animishadēva was his Guru and himself the disciple.

Because Animishadēva could not interact with Prabhudeva for the physical process of initiation, the initiation takes place only through the mental process effected through mere will.

Prabhudeva, here, describes the fundamental tenet of the Oneness Philosophy. Though Prabhudeva and Animishadēva appear to be different from the physical point of view, they are identical (one and the same) from the spiritual point of view. **For the thorough-going monist the Reality is beyond duality; it is only 'One'.** For the one who is well advanced in one's spiritual attainment, when the certitude that one's own-Self is the Absolute is attained, that knowledge itself becomes the Guru. Here, Prabhudeva is pointing out that for those who are well advanced in their spiritual attainment, there is no need for an external physical Guru.

Vachana 36 on pages 85 and 86 of volume I of Shunya Sampadane (1) is as follows:

Do I say one? It is as two!
Do I say two? It is really one!
Why, then, this question of one or two?
Can you conceive indivisible union without grace indivisible?
Disciple and Master know no division
O Guheshvara.

Thus Prabhudeva feels no difference between Guru and disciple in his case, and decides to receive the grace as if he were the Guru himself. After bowing down to the holy feet of Animishadēva, Prabhudeva picks up the Ishtalinga from the palm of Animishadēva. At that instant, Animishadēva attains the Absolute Shunya, and his body falls down to the ground. Prabhudeva, instantly receives the grace of Guru by mere will.

The mental-type process of initiation is meant only for the ones who are at a higher plane of consciousness and are well advanced in their spiritual attainment. For them there is no need for an external physical Guru. In this context, Prabhudeva describes the process of obtaining initiation in one of his vachanas. Vachana 37 on pages 86 and 87 of volume I of Shunya Sampadane (1) is as follows:

Should the master you never hoped to see
Appears before your eyes,
What need of utterance to your worship?
What need of touching to your touch?
What need of ash-mark's smear?
What need the whispered mantra in your ear?
The holy water need never flow,
And for your initiation
No chapter and verse of Scripture be intoned.
Here you have the Linga without worship,
A bond without binding,
Oh, make me, O Guheshvara,
Fit to receive Thy fitting grace.

When the invisible Guru is visualized, there is no obeisance, there is no touching of the head, there is no smearing of the sacred ash, there is no whispered mantra in the ear, and there is no sprinkling of the holy water; the scripture is not intoned, there is no ritualistic worship of Ishtalinga, and there is bond without binding.

The other type of initiation, involving the physical process, is said to be for the ordinary aspirants who are in a lower plane of consciousness. This physical process is carried out by the Guru. It involves rites and rituals such as besmearing the body with sacred ash, placing the palm on the disciple's head, whispering the mantra into the disciple's ear, and investing the Ishtalinga on the seeker's palm.

Guru is a master of spiritual knowledge who has realized the state of identity with Linga. Guru instills spiritual knowledge into the disciple. An aspirant who yearns for self-realization is impelled to seek a competent Guru. The seeking and striving of the disciple goes on until the aspirant reaches the spiritual that takes the form of Linga. To such a seeker whose mind is peaceful and controlled, the learned Guru imparts the knowledge of the Absolute in its very essence, the knowledge by which one knows the true imperishable Being.

The process of initiation performed by the Guru is said to accomplish the following. First the disciple is purified of the three impurities or taints: impurity *(āṇavamala)* that subsists in the soul and keeps the soul separated from the Divine; impurity *(Māyāmala)* associated with Māyā which keeps the soul ignorant of its own nature; and the taint *(kārmikamala)* associated with the individual souls which enjoy or suffer according to their deeds.

It is to be emphasized here, that these three impurities are not in the Supreme Divine, they get attached to the soul during the creation; the impurities need to be eliminated in order to attain oneness with the Divine.

Next there is Divine descent into the mind, life and matter in the form of Linga. The path of the miraculous Linga coming to the palm and its effect of making one passion-free is explained by Allama Prabhudeva in one of his vachanas.

Vachana 44 on pages 94 and 95 in volume I of Shunya Sampadane (1) is something like this:

Instead of the Unseen,
Should you seek the seen?
That which is greater than the Great
Has itself become the Guru,
Has itself become the Linga,
Itself the Jangama and the Grace,
Itself the end and the means
Of the miraculous path,
Itself the embodiment of all knowledge;
When 'That' which has grown into All,
Now sits upon my palm,
Henceforth I shall be passion-free,
O Guheshvara!

In the above vachana, Prabhudeva is saying that the Divine itself becomes Guru the preceptor, Linga the principle, Jangama the person, Vidya the knowledge, Prasada the grace, and Mantra the power. Thus, it is said that **love, knowledge, power, bliss and peace are the radiant expressions of the Divine.** With this Divine descent, the person is passion-free.

This mere sight of the Divine is not enough to be united with the Divine. The seeker must then ascend to attain oneness.

Bhaktasthala

After the above preliminary sthalas, Bhaktasthala is described in only three vachanas in Shunya Sampadane.

The mere sight of the Divine is not enough to be united with the Divine. The seeker must then ascend to attain oneness.

The disciple has to understand that the light of knowledge shines by means of devotion. Thence the seeker will develop intense devotion to attain this knowledge. Vachana 56 on page 104 in volume I of Shunya Sampadane (1) is as follows:

Here is the earthen lamp
And here is the wick
Bu how can this be waving of an oil-less light?
The Master is here and the Linga too is here.
But yet, until the light of knowledge dawns
Into the votary's heart
How can devotion shine?
I disown him should he decline to serve
Having heard the Heavenly voice,
O Guheshvara.

The earthen lamp and the wick are here but there is no oil. Without oil you cannot light the lamp. Guru invests the Linga upon the disciple, but the devotion does not shine until the light of knowledge dawns into the disciple's heart.

Devotee's daily life includes worship of Linga in the morning, performing dedicated work, serving the community and treating everyone with respect and humility.

Daily duties are explained in vachana 58 on page 105 in volume I of Shūnya Sampādane; it is as follows:

To supplicate the Liṅga in the early hours;
To greet the saints of Shiva at early dawn –
This is the worth of life!
Thus says the scriptural word.
I dislike those who do not honor such,
O Guheshvara.

Worship of Linga, unconditional service to Guru, and self-dedication to Jangama are the principal features of this stage. Bhaktasthala teaches one to incorporate austerity, restraint and dedicated work in one's daily life.

Bhakti denotes the concept of devotee and the Divine; it implies duality. This has to be reckoned with. Sharanas are monists (non-dualists). They believe in only one Reality. They preferentially use the term ***'Sad-bhakti'*** which means ***'true devotion'***.

In order to overcome this duality situation, Sharanas have adopted what is recommended in the Upanishads (14):

- It is said in the discussion part of Kena Upanishad (page 10 of reference 16) that devotion is of two types. The first type is the devotion that is an expression of the knowledge of unity. This type of devotion is practiced by the wise who already have realized the 'unity'. The realization is that, one's own-Self and God adored as the creator of the universe, are the manifestations of the same basic reality that is Brahman. In the state of relative consciousness, one adores God in ecstatic love; this is identical with the Knowledge. Thus one exhibits Devine expression of love, knowledge, power, bliss and peace. The other type of devotion is the devotion that leads to that knowledge. In this type of devotion the aspirant has not attained the knowledge of unity, and therefore cannot yet express it. Thus the devotion is a matter of faith and not of expression. To attain that knowledge, the devotee worships God externally; it stimulates Divine love that rouses Ātman-consciousness. The above discussion comes about for the explanation of Kena Upanishad (16) mantras I.5-9. **Bhaktasthala is about this second type of devotion that leads to the attainment of the knowledge of unity.**

- Furthermore, Kena Upanishad (16) mantra IV.8 says something like *'Austerity, restraint, and dedicated work are the three means to that end, and as such, are included in the Upanishad'.*
- Bhaktasthala teaches one to incorporate austerity, restraint and dedicated work in one's life.
- Mantra II.7 of Shvetashvatara-Upanishad (9) says that *one should be devoted to that ancient Brahman - towards the Immanent Soul*

conceived as the Prime Cause.

- Explanation for this passage on page 45 of reference 9 is as follows. The Absolute is beyond thought and speech, and cannot be the subject of devotion. Devotion requires the duality of devotee and the Divine. Therefore to approach the unity of the Absolute through some best possible form of devotion is that towards the immanent Ātman conceived as the Prime Cause, whose presence is felt by all devotees in their hearts. Because the Absolute cannot be the subject of devotion and cannot be devoted to directly, one has to conceive the concept of the Creator and show devotion to the Prime Cause.

The above teachings in the Upanishads have profoundly influenced the development of Bhaktasthala of the Sharanas.

In Bhaktasthala the seeker develops intense devotion to attain the knowledge, and then moves on to the next stage where the devotee develops firm conviction in the faith of Linga.

Māheshvarasthala

The one who already has intense devotion, develops firm conviction in the faith of Linga.

Māheshvarasthala is described in four vachanas in Shunya Sampadane. The teaching in the vachanas is as follows:

The true-devotee understands that one who wavers and entertains the desire for another god or gods is neither brave nor resolute, and thus, by understanding that, the true-devotee develops steadfastness of faith in Linga.

This above point is depicted in one of Allama Prabhudeva's vachanas. Vachana 59 on page 106 in volume I of reference 1 is something like this:

They who cannot ride a ready horse
Yet ask for another one
Are neither brave nor resolute.
Therefore, through the three worlds
They labor and sweat
Carrying the saddle on their back
O Guheshvara!

Most of Allama Prabhudeva's vachanas are enigmatic and difficult to understand. In the above vachana 'cannot ride a ready horse' means 'cannot accept the concept that there is only one God'. Such ones revolve in the cycle of births and deaths without advancing spiritually.

Maheshvara clears the eight-fold taints of earth, water, fire, air, sky, moon, sun, and ego. Prabhudēva's vachana 60 on pages 106 and 107 in volume I of Shūnya Sampādane (1) makes this point:

We are pious, we are pious, they cry!
But, I am shocked to see
The self-styled devotees who worship
The Liṅga without clearing the taint of
Earth and water, of fire, and air, and sky,
Of sun and moon, and of self (ego)
O Guheshvara.

It is said that the phenomenal nature Prakriti is considered impure by the Veerashaivas, and that the evolutes of Prakriti named above are also impure – taints that are to be cleared off of the person.

Maheshvara intensifies the worship of Linga.

Removal of doubt and misgivings, and development of full confidence in Linga worship, enhances the depth of devotion.

As devotion becomes intense, rites and rituals are dispensed with, and the internal worship is developed. The silent contemplation of the Divine remains the only yearning.

Shvetashvatara-Upanishad (9) mantras III.1-2 speak of the oneness of the Ultimate

Reality despite its apparent diversity in functions, and imply that only this Reality is to be known:

'One who exists alone during the time of creation and dissolution of the universe, by virtue of its inscrutable power assumes manifold powers, and appears as the Divine Lord who protects all the worlds and controls all the forces working there off. That is indeed one only. O people, He is present inside the hearts of all beings. One who worships Him only, and realizes this 'Being', becomes immortal.'

As one becomes unwaveringly vigilant in the steadfastness, one advances to the next stage of one's spiritual journey.

Prasādisthala

In this Prasādisthala, one exhibits attentiveness or careful vigilance in one's dedication. Anything dedicated with sincerity and without reservations will become Prasada. One who dedicates it is a Prasadi. Prasada that ensues is calmness, tranquility, serenity and such. **The mental sign that shows purity is Prasada.**

It is generally believed that a food item, a piece of coconut-kernel or a fruit, consecrated by Guru, Linga or Jangama, is Prasada that is to be consumed. That may be a common meaning, but it is not the true meaning of Prasada.

In one of his vachanas, Allama Prabhudeva says that Prasadi is one who understands the true meaning of the tie uniting what is served, what is left over, what is consumed, and such. Vachana on page 11 in volume I of Shunya Sampadane (1) is something like this:

They call what is served as Prasada,
They call what is left over as Prasada,
But even the cat accepts these served
And left over things.
The one who has understood
The five links that bind these is
The Prasadi in Guheshvara-Linga.

The term 'Prasada', in general, means 'grace' which is explained as a virtue coming from God to the devotee. This type of explanation implies duality where God and the devotee are two separate entities. The aspirant has not completely transited from the apparent duality to oneness while treading in the Prasadisthala. Therefore, the explanation may imply duality, but it really is the oneness philosophy.

One, whose pure mind is always absorbed in the Linga, experiences the state of non-duality.

In Shunya Sampadane, Prasadisthala is described in three vachanas.

One dedicates oneself as the offering to the Divine. One, who, by offering the body, mind and will, to Guru, Linga and Jangama, achieves purity of the body, clarity of the mind, and perfection of the will. That one is the partaker of the grace of the Divine that is Prasada. Everything is offered with a sense of self-dedication and self-surrender.

Allama Prabhudeva gives this information stated above, in one of his vachanas. Vachana 63 on page 109 in volume I of Shunya Sampadane (1) is something like this:

Whether the Three are eternal
Or the Three are not eternal
Who can tell?
By providing three services to the Three,
If one gains the three Prasādas,
That one is the Lord of the Three
The brave, the resolute
And a Prasadi in Guheshvara-Linga.

The term *'trividha'* which means *'trinity'* comes six times in this vachana. The eternal three refers to Guru, Linga and Jangama. The three services are worship of Linga, unconditional service to Guru, and self-dedication to Jangama. The three types of Prasāda are – Shuddha (pure) Prasāda, Siddha (perfect) Prasāda, and the Prasiddha (renowned) Prasāda.

The offerings are to be free from any taint. If attachment or craving persists, the transformation to Prasada will not be effected. When ignorance and the sense of ego are completely eliminated, and the offering is made with sincerity and humility, Prasada ensues, and poise and peace are attained by the devotee. Serenity is characteristic of the Prasadi.

Thus, when it is offered properly, the fire of knowledge burns the illusion of desire into an illumination of joy.

True Prasada is **'serenity'** that ensues when one completely eliminates ignorance and sense of ego. Prasada, the peace of mind, is necessary for one to advance further in one's spiritual progress.

Prāṇaliṅgisthala

From the Bhaktasthala to the Prasādisthala, the concept of duality progresses to the concept of non-duality (oneness). And from Prāṇaliṅgisthala onwards, it is all oneness philosophy.

'Prāṇa' means *'breath of life'* in general. It is also referred to as life, life-force, life-energy, vital breath, and such. Prana sometimes gets confused with 'Jiva'. Prana is not Jiva; Jiva is soul. Prana is not soul. Prana is born out of Ātman. It is like the shadow of the Ātman, and has no separate existence (18).

Prāṇa is the universal energy or the cosmic power that is confined in the body. Prana carries out the physical functions of the body. Without Prana the person/body dies. Prana is responsible for all the life forces that make the embodiment of the Divine possible

Prāṇa refers to the vital energy in a person, and Linga is enshrined in the person's body. Through breath-control *(prāṇāyāma),* one can make this vital energy get absorbed into the Linga. During this process one ignores the external world and focuses on the internal Linga. **One who withdraws from outer objects and concentrates on the internal Linga is a *'Prāṇaliṅgi'*.**

In Shunya Sampadane, Pranalingisthala is described in three vachanas. The first of the three vachanas needs detailed discussion which is given below after the vachana itself. Vachana 66 in this first chapter, on pages 111 and 112 in volume I is as follows:

Water taking form arose in the body.
The pedestal got installed in my body
The city of Shiva.
The breath becoming worshipper,
Tying a fragrant bouquet,
Was worshipping in the
Prime-middle-station of
The nine-door-Shiva-shrine.
Linga called Guheshvara was standing there!

Details of the discussion are as follows:

- In the above vachana, it is not clear what Prabhudeva means when he says *'water (udaka) taking form arose in the body'*. It may mean the water of pāda-udaka (Pādōdaka). The common meaning of Pādōdaka is the water that has washed the feet of Guru and Jangama, and also the water that has washed the Ishtalinga. In the Sharana concept, the meaning of **Pādōdaka is 'Bliss'** that flows like water from the Divine to the Sharana.
- The vachana states that the base/pedestal got installed in my body, and uses the term *'Mūlasthāna'* which means base (Mūla is root, and sthāna is station or place).

- The body is referred to as the *city of Shiva*, and also as a *nine-door Shiva-shrine*. The city of Shiva is the same as the Upanishads' description of the body as *'the City of Brahman'*. In this vachana the body is referred to as the nine-door-shrine; it is also similar to the *nine-gate-city of Brahman* that comes in Shvetashvatara Upanishad III.18 (9), and also the eleven-gate-city given in Katha Upanishad V.1 (10). The 11 gates are: two eyes, two ears, two nostrils, one mouth, two excretory openings, the navel, and Brahmarandhra at the top of the head. Nine gates are the above eleven without the two gates - navel and Brahmarandhra.
- *'Breath becoming worshipper'* in the vachana refers to breath control – pranayama. Shvetashvatara Upanishad II.9 (9) points out that breath control is to be practiced after calming all the activities including that of the mind.
- The Kannada term *'Ādimadhyasthānadalli'* is singular; it refers to one station *(sthāna)*. The term 'Ādi (pronounced as Aadi)' is explained in Chāndogya Upanishad (13) II.8.1 to mean 'the first' or 'the beginning of all', and 'Ādi' is said to mean the syllable 'Om'. Madhya means middle. This 'prime-middle-station' refers to the **heart** as in the Upanishads.
- Linga was standing there in the heart!
- The breath, when regulated, emits fragrance for the worship of Linga enshrined in the body.

However, it is to be pointed out that the explanation given by the editors of volume I of Shunya Sampadane is different from what is given above. The names of the editors of volume I are different from those of the other volumes as given in the article 'Shūnya Sampādane Texts' in this book. The editor's explanation is on pages 404 and 405 of volume I. The editors explain this vachana using the Kundalini-Yoga components; the editors' explanation is not acceptable. Sharanas do not practice Kundalini-Yoga of the Tantra Philosophy. The reasons for this disagreement are as follows:

- Although it is not clear what Prabhudeva means when he uses the term water, it probably means the water of Padodaka. The meaning of the Veerashaiva Padodaka is 'Bliss' that flows like water from the Divine to the devotee. This water becomes Linga in the body. But the editors call this water 'life-force' which means Prana; it is not acceptable.
- The Kannada word *'mūruti'* means form, but the editors say it is Kundalini. The editors state that Prana took form as Kundalini. This is not acceptable at all. In Kundalini-Yoga, Prana and Kundalini are two separate energies. Prana does not become Kundalini. Prana is a dynamic form of energy that sustains life, and Kundalini is a potential type of energy which stays dormant. When activated, Kundalini is much more powerful energy than Prana. These two are separate - one does not become the other.

- The vachana states that the base/pedestal got installed in my body, and uses the term *'Mūlasthāna'* which means base or pedestal. The editors say that it means 'Ādhāra-chakra' where Kundalini lies coiled up. It is not the case.
- The term *'Ādimadhyasthānadalli'* is singular; it refers to one sthāna/station, not to two chakras. Madhya means middle. This prime-middle-station refers to the heart as in the Upanishads. The editors say the above singular term refers to two of the seven chakras of Kundalini-Yoga. This is not acceptable.
- At the end of their note, to support their contention, they give Siddhānta Shikhāmaṇi (6) reference XII.13-20 which, of course, does not have anything about Kundalini. Translation of the Siddhānta Shikhāmaṇi verses referred to above, is given here in brief: *'Pranalinga should be conceived as seated on the lotus-seat in the temple of the heart which is pervaded by the inner vital breath...'*

Shunya Sampadane makes it very clear that Veerashaivas do not practice Kundalini-Yoga. This discussion is in two of its chapters, both related to the great Shivayogi Siddharāmayya. Details are in those two chapters to come later in this book.

It is to be pointed out that the editors of volume III, not editors of volume I, of the referenced Shunya Sampadane (1), on pages 412 and 413 of volume III, state that Prabhudeva advises Siddharamayya as:

"In order to confirm oneself in this faith (Veerashaiva faith), one must discard one's belief in the traditional ways prescribed by the scriptures, such as yogic concentration and practice of the Kundalini method".

Thus, the editors of volume III of the referenced Shunya Sampadane (1) make it clear that Veerashaivas do not practice Kundalini-Yoga. (Names of the editors of the five volumes differ, and are given in the article 'Shunya Sampadane' in this book.)

Furthermore, Allama Prabhudeva has vachanas about *'Ashṭāṅga Yoga'* which is also called as *'Raja Yoga'*. The eight steps of this Yoga are *yama, niyama, asana, pranayama, pratyahara, dharana, dhyana, and samadhi.* Prabhudeva promotes the practice of this Raja Yoga. Pranayama is part of this yoga. Thus, pranayama applicable in this situation is given below in this book.

Continuing on, in the Pranalingisthala one ignores the external world and focuses on the internal Linga that is enshrined in the body. One who withdraws from outer objects and concentrates on the internal Linga is a Pranalingi. Conscious Self-experience is the main characteristic of Pranalingisthala. The seeker's vision tends inwards and gets clarified. The breath, when regulated, emits fragrance for the Linga enshrined in the body.

Allama Prabhudēva describes the experience of a Prāṇaliṅgi during the internal worship of Liṅga in his vachana 67 on page 112 in volume I of Shūnya Sampādane; it is as follows:

Unimaginable the light in the eyes!
Indescribable the ring in the ear!
Incomparable the taste on the tongue!
Immeasurable the peace
Of the inconceivable Sushumnā nāḍi!
Everywhere you will find Him:
In the minutest particles of dust,
In hard wood, or tender blade of grass.
Everywhere He is!
The subtle, the imperishable,
The unchanging Guheshvara!

To explain the second part of the above vachana, the editors quote the transliterated second half of verse II.20 from Katha Upanishad. Here it is translated as follows (10):

That desire-less one, being free from grief, realizes that glory of Ātman through the purity of sense and mind.

For some reason the editors left out the first half of the verse II.20 from Katha Upanishad (10) which is something like this:

Ātman, smaller than the smallest, and greater than the greatest, dwells in the hearts of creatures.

The first part of the above vachana is similar to the description in Shvetāshvatara Upanishad (9) verse II.11 where mental modifications occurring during yoga practice is given. It is as follows:

Forms that appear like snow, smoke, sun, wind, fire, fire-fly, lightening, crystal, and moon, precede the manifestation of Brahman in Yoga practice.

Experiences of Pranalingi in the Pranalingisthala in the form of flashes and streams of sensations, mentioned above are said to be intermittent. When these experiences become steady, and are replaced by the 'Self' seeing its own light shining in Divine splendor, the Prāṇaliṅgi moves on to the next stage of Sharaṇasthala.

The practice of pranayama that is applicable in this situation is given in the article 'Pranayama'.

Prāṇāyāma

Prāṇāyāma, pronounced as praaṇaayaama, is the complete control and distribution of vital energy in the body by means of regulation of breathing.

Prāṇa means life-energy. Prana is not the soul. Prana is born out of Ātman. It is like the shadow of the Ātman, and has no separate existence. Prana is the universal energy or the cosmic power that is confined in the body. Prana carries out the physical functions of the body. Without Prana the person/body dies. Prana is responsible for all the life forces that make the embodiment of the Divine possible.

Prāṇa flows through conduits in the body. The conduit or the channel through which the Prāṇa moves is called an nāḍi (it is called nāḷa in Kannaḍa). The nāḍis of the Veerashaivas are the same as those described in the Upanishads (not of the Tantra literature). The nāḍis radiate out going from the heart to all parts of the body. This may imply that the nāḍis are blood vessels not the nerves. Prana and the conduits were visualized during yogic meditation by the ancient sages at the time when anatomical nerves and blood-vessels were not clearly understood by them.

It is to be pointed out to the readers that the main channel/conduit called the Sushumnā nāḍi mentioned above in vachana 67 of Prabhudeva, goes from the heart to the top of the head (but, in the Tantra system which does not apply to the Veerashaivas, it goes from Mūlādhāra chakra located at the level of coccyx at the lower end of the spine to the top of the head).

Expression of Prana is through breathing. While Prana is linked to this vital function of the body, it is not the breath itself. During the performance of Pranayama, the flow of energy in the body is regulated and controlled by **fine, deep and rhythmic breathing** (19). While there are many techniques of performance of pranayama, the following type is practiced by the Veerashaivas.

Pranayama is to be practiced only in its elementary form. It is performed while the person is seated comfortably in the yoga-meditation position. Simple posture for yoga-meditation that can be held for a sufficient time, without any discomfort, is the sitting position. One should have a seat which is neither too hard nor too soft. The correct posture is to sit straight and cross-legged with eyes looking straight out and hands resting on the lap. For some individuals, sitting cross-legged may not be comfortable; for them, sitting on a chair with legs down resting on the floor is acceptable.

Every aspect of breath-control is performed in a relaxed manner, and there should not be any jerky/sudden movement. **Fine breathing** is a noiseless breathing through both nostrils. It is not breathing through one nostril and then the other. **Deep-rhythmic breathing** is not deep-rapid breathing which may lead to complications.

There are three aspects – inhalation, exhalation, and retention. Inhalation is accomplished by taking in a large breath of air smoothly. Exhalation of the breath is gradual, relaxed and smooth. Retention of the breath occurs twice, once at the end of inhalation, and then at the end of exhalation. End-inhalation breath-hold is not natural because the breathing muscles are not relaxed. It should not be forced. If stability of the breath-hold is lost, the breath has to be released. Duration of this retention of the breath is what is comfortable for that person. End-exhalation breath-hold is natural because all the muscles are relaxed then. The duration of this retention is also what is comfortable for the individual. One should not focus on the time it takes to inhale, exhale or to hold the breath. Rhythmicity gets established naturally on the basis of the body's needs. During this process of breath regulation, one feels a gradual expansion of the chest, and feels the air reaching all parts of the lungs.

This process of breath regulation moves life-energy throughout the body. The energy is distributed throughout the body via the innumerable conduits (energy passageways). Breath-control directly affects the ascending and descending currents of life-force. In an ordinary individual, the currents exist in a haphazard manner, and pose as obstacles for a free flow of vital-energy. The yogic meditative practice of self-purification places these currents in a proper order of alignment.

Breath-control, as practiced by Veerashaivas, is applicable not only for spiritual fitness but also for physical and mental fitness. Specifically, mental calmness ensues from this practice. This technique does not lead to any type of respiratory or gas exchange complication. Some other techniques such as breathing rapidly and excessively (hyperventilating) and then holding the breath may lead to serious complications. Breathing is a vital function; one cannot live without it. The Veerashaiva technique changes the pattern of breathing to achieve mental calmness and focus, without interfering with the homeostatic mechanisms of the body.

Once the fine, deep and rhythmical breathing is established, the focus is changed from breath control to meditation while maintaining such breathing.

Sharaṇasthala

Sharaṇa is the one who is characterized by pure delight *(Ānanda)* that is derived from contemplation on the inner Linga/Self. Ānanda, the Joy of Divine Consciousness is the hallmark of this sthala. One develops awareness within that Conscious Self-experience of the Prāṇaliṅgi.

Experiences of Pranalingi in the Pranalingisthala in the form of intermittent flashes and streams of sensations are replaced in this Sharanasthala by the 'Self' seeing its own light shining in Divine splendor (1).

In order to accomplish this state, one has to continue to contemplate on the inner Self/Linga. As a result of deep and intense meditation, the Divine Light shines inward, and a joyful serene mood springs up.

Sharanasthala is described in three vachanas in Shunya Sampadane.

In one of his vachanas, Allama Prabhudeva describes what occurs during continued contemplation. As a result of continued contemplation on the inner Self, all memory dies, all error burns, awareness gets forgotten, all symbols crumble, body's motion ceases, and the mind gets lost in the Linga. Vachana 69 on gages 113 and 114 in volume I of Shunya Sampadane (1) is as follows:

All memory is dead; all error burnt;

Awareness is forgotten;
All symbols have crumbled.
Where is now motion or mind?
There is no motion, no mind,
Nor the body, for it is lost in the Linga;
Gone too
All that came between the eyes and light
O Guheshvara!

As a result of continued contemplation on the inner Self, all memory is dead, all error burnt, awareness forgotten, all symbols have crumbled, there is no motion for the body, and the mind gets lost in the Linga.

It may be interesting to the readers to note that the above vachana information is comparable to part of a mantra in Brihadaranyaka Upanishad IV.3.21 which says something like this (8):

'...this infinite entity (the individual-self) fully embraced by Pure Consciousness of the Supreme-Self, knows nothing external or internal...'

When the mind with attributes as well as the mind without attributes stops, the silence reigns. When consciousness of being oneself ends, the ecstasy (Ānanda) dwells. Sharana beholds the light of the Linga as a resplendent blaze. Allama Prabhudeva's vachana gives this information. Vachana 70 on pages 114 and 115 in volume I of Shunya Sampadane (1) is something like this:

Where the mind

Conditioned and unconditioned stops,
There, silence reigns.
Where consciousness of being oneself
Reaches an end-point
There, ecstasy dwells.
I have beheld the light of the Linga
As a resplendent blaze, O Guheshvara!

Constant contemplation on the inner Linga results in Bliss, which is Ānanda.

- Katha Upanishad (10) VI.11 says something like *'Firm control of the senses and fixing the mind in contemplation is known as Yoga. The person who performs the Yoga, the Yogin, must not allow the mind to wander from object to object by inefficient control of the mind, but must make the mind steady in concentration; the Yogin then becomes free from the vagueness of the mind'.*
- And then in V.13-14 the Katha Upanishad (10) says *'The wise who perceive the eternal, the intelligence in the intelligent, as existing within their own self, to them belongs eternal peace, and to none else. The sages perceive that indescribable Joy of the Supreme as 'this is that''.*
- Chāndogya-Upanishad (13) VII.23.1 says *'That which is Infinite alone is happiness'.*

Then there is this enigmatic vachana of Allama Prabhudeva about an important concept. It states that there is a head above another head, and that the head above swallows the head below. These two heads are said to refer to two kinds of knowledge. The two heads may also refer to the two consciousness states – Individual Consciousness, and the Supreme Consciousness. Vachana 71 on page 115 in volume I of Shunya Sampadane (1) is something like this:

Above a head there is a head;
The head above
Has swallowed the head below.
Tell me, if one can drink milk being dead,
And what links up the two!
I have seen in Thee
The joy a child finds in a dream
O Guheshvara!

These two heads refer to two kinds of knowledge – a higher supra-mental knowledge and a lower empirical knowledge. The empirical knowledge resolves into supra-mental knowledge, and the sense of duality is replaced by the knowledge of significance of the Union. It also means that the lower individual consciousness is taken over by the upper Supra-Conscious state. The seeker experiences Ānanda/Bliss.

What is in the above vachana is a very important concept; it comes in many Upanishads.

In Muṇḍaka Upanishad (20), first there is a question in mantra I.1.3:

'What is that by knowing which everything becomes known?'

Then the answer is given in mantras I.1.4 and I.1.5:

'There are two kinds of knowledge that are to be acquired. One is a lower knowledge, and the other is a higher knowledge. The lower knowledge consists of the study of the Vedas and everything else that is attained through the senses. The higher knowledge is that by which the Absolute is attained'.

In Brihadāraṇyaka Upanishad (8) passage II.4.12, Yajnavalkya, the compiler of Shukla Yajurveda, in continuing to teach his wife, says:

'As a lump of salt thrown into water dissolves in it and whichever part of water sampled has only the saline taste, so also the great, endless, infinite Reality is only homogeneous Intelligence. On account of the elements of the body, the individual-self stands out separately, but as soon as these elements are destroyed, the separate existence is also destroyed. After attaining the higher Knowledge, there is no separate existence'.

Thus, in Sharanasthala, all memory dies, all error burns, awareness gets forgotten, all symbols crumble, body's motion ceases, and the mind gets lost in the Linga. The individual consciousness is taken over by the Supra-mental Consciousness.

Aikyasthala

The Sharana of Sharanasthala, who attains identity with the Absolute by becoming one with it, becomes an Aikya in this very life.

Shunya Sampadane (1) gives this following information:

Becoming a Bhakta by one's own faith,
Becoming a Maheshvara by steadfastness in that faith,
Becoming a Prasadi by vigilance in that steadfastness,
Becoming a Pranalingi by self-experience in that vigilance,
Becoming a Sharana by awareness in that self-experience,
Then becomes an Aikya by the mystery abiding in a state of will-less-ness when that awareness merges in the Truth.

Aikyasthala is described in three vachanas.

One vachana, explains that an Aikya has no word to describe the achievement. Vachana 72 in this chapter one is something like this:

The motion of the will is still!
All sound is dedicated offering, you see!
When the sound called Guheshvara
Becomes Knowledge,
The word has no trace of sound,
Nor is there in all space a bound!

There is no volition, no motion, no word or speech, and there is no consciousness of time and space. It is the Absolute Knowledge.

In another vachana Allama Prabhudeva describes this Aikya state, saying that there is only one consciousness. There is no separate consciousness of the individual. In this Supra-Conscious state, if one would see, will not see, and if one would hear, cannot hear. The one has reached true Reality – It is indescribable, and the great white light is everywhere. Vachana 73 on page 117 in volume I of Shunya Sampadane (1) is something like this:

O Lord, I have been in reality beyond conceit
Called Nirvikalpa (no self-consciousness)!
If I would see, I do not see,
If I would hear, I cannot hear.
O Guheshvara,
The great white Light is everywhere!

Here the Self is absorbed in the intense and focused meditation on the transcendent passing over the limits of mind and entering into the ecstatic state. This Aikya state is the attainment of **Nirvikalpa Samādhi**, an indeterminate trance, where there is no separate consciousness of the individual. It is only the Supra-Conscious state. There is no residue of any kind of the individual-self in the Supra-Conscious state. This Supreme state is not conscious of anything. This is the highest level of attainment of Oneness, and it is to be known only. To attain it, one has to focus on nothing but the contemplation on the Self which is Shunya. Somewhat of a lower type of Samadhi may result if there is some retention of the self-volition when absorbed into the super-conscious state.

Allama Prabhudeva describes an 'Aikya', the one who has attained the Aikya-state in his vachana. Vachana 74 on pages 117 and 118 in volume I of Shunya Sampadane (1) is as follows:

One who, having known Reality, is past care;
The hero, vanquisher of death;
The glorious, embodiment of the Most High;
The blessed, who has attained the Bliss;
The perfect who inhabits the Void (Bayalu);
The self-begot who has attained
Tranquil Guheshvara-Linga.

Six characteristics of an Aikya given in the above vachana are explained in Shunya Sampadane as follows (1):

- *The one who, having known The Reality, is past care:* Once the Truth is known and realized as an experience, there is no changeable state such as a sense of worry, anxiety and such; there is only calm vision and tranquility.

- *The Hero, vanquisher of death:* One has become immortal in the sense that the Consciousness is beyond the chain of cause and effect, and beyond the cycle of births and deaths.
- *The Glorious, embodiment of the Most High:* The Glorious one has the direct vision of the Supreme. It perceives the soul in all beings to be its own – it is the vision of the Self in all and all in the Self.
- *The Blessed, who has attained the Bliss:* Consequent to the transformation of the human nature into the divine nature, the Blessed one has attained the state of Blissful Consciousness.
- *The Perfect, who inhabits the Void:* Perfection has been attained and the Perfect one is Shunya/Bayalu.
- *The self-begot, who has attained the Perfect Poise:* The Spontaneous one is the supernal conscious being with Perfect Composure.

An Aikya is described as – the knower of the truth, has become immortal, is sublime and of the most-high, has attained Bliss, is an inhabitant of the Void, and perfect and serene. Having gone through the spiritual hierarchy of Shatsthala, the seeker has attained oneness. This attainment while still alive is the liberation in life called Jivanmukti.

Some of these concepts are from the Upanishads (14):

- Muṇḍaka Upanishad (20) III.2.8-9 says something like *'As flowing rivers loose name and form when they disappear in the ocean, even so the wise one free from name and form goes into the highest of the high – the Supreme Divinity. Whoever knows the Supreme Brahman becomes the very Brahman'.*

- Taittirīya-Upanishad (21) II.1 has a similar statement *'one who realizes Brahman attains the Supreme'.*
- Somewhat similar statement is in Brihadaranyaka Upanishad (8) IV.4.6 which says something like *'One who has no craving, whose only object of desire is the Self, being Brahman itself, is merged in Brahman'.*
- Brihadāraṇyaka Upanishad (8), in II.3.1-6 states that Brahman has only two limiting adjuncts superimposed on it through ignorance – gross and subtle forms... But the specification about Brahman is *'not this, not this'*, eliminating not only the two limiting adjuncts, gross and subtle forms stated above, but also all possible specification about Brahman. There is no other or better specification than 'not this, not this'. Its sacred name is Truth of truth.

Having gone through the spiritual hierarchy of **Shaṭsthala**, the seeker has attained oneness. This attainment while still alive is the liberation in life called the Jīvanmukti state, and the one who has attained this state is a Jīvanmukta.

JAṄGAMASTHALA

Jaṅgama is the one who has attained oneness with the Absolute Divine by going through the six stages of Shatsthala. Jangama is a Jīvanmukta, the one who has been liberated from the cycle of births and deaths. Being liberated in this very life, Jangama still has the body. Wearing the body as garment, Jangama continues to serve humanity. This Jangama state is called **Jaṅgama-sthala**.

Shunya Sampadane (1) describes Jangamasthala as the ultimate sthala. The Jangamasthala represents the final consummation of a seeker who has absorbed the Divine. This sthala signifies the state of one who, having attained oneness with the Absolute, is able to revitalize society.

Shunya Sampadane describes Jangamasthala in four vachanas.

The seventy-fifth vachana in the first chapter of Shunya Sampadane is a long one. It is an obeisance to the one who has realized The Reality. Obeisance means homage, deference, reverential regard, submission, bow down to show respect, and such. Obeisance is not prayer.

The vachana begins with the use of figurative language to describe the Jangama – '*To the Glorious One who moves about in the effulgent light and radiance and splendor of knowledge, and such'*. Then it gives the mode of internal subjective worship conducted through exaltation of the will. And ends with *'To the Glorious One who has realized The Reality, obeisance, obeisance!'*

In another vachana Allama Prabhudeva describes how, one who has attained such a Jangama state, goes wandering about in order to bless the cohorts of all the Ancients. Vachana 76 on page 123 in volume I of Shunya Sampadane (1) is as follows:

Show me the Supreme Lord whose
Gait is without feet, whose
Touch is without hands, whose
Taste is without tongue, who requests
With a bowl of Love for the Supreme,
O Guheshvara!

Jangama walks without feet, touches without palm, tastes without tongue, and makes the feeling itself request earnestly for supreme felicity – the unreserved surrender to the Supreme. **It should be noted that this is not begging for ordinary alms.**

Jangama moves for the redemption of mankind, and blesses the aspirants by mere will. With illumined knowledge and enlightened action, the great one acts as a source of Divine Grace.

The last vachana in this chapter describes the effects of Oneness transformation:

Vachana 78 on page 124 in volume I of Shunya Sampadane (1), as translated there, is given below:

Incomparable is the beauty of your going:
It alchemizes all that is touched;
It consecrates all that is seen;
It turns all that is heard
Into spiritual discourse;
They are forthwith saved,
Who hold converse with you!
You purify the world as you pass by;
Each spot you tread is a pilgrim place;
The waters you touch are holy waters;
And all those who pledge devotion to you
Became one with you,
O Guheshvara!

Whatever the Jangama touches, gets alchemized. [The Kannaḍa term 'paruṣa (ಪರುಷ)' which means alchemy comes frequently in the vachanas. Alchemy is a mediaeval chemistry: everything was thought to be possible. Alchemy is a power to transform something common to something precious: like transforming iron to gold.] Whatever Jangama sees, becomes consecrated. Whatever that is heard from Jangama, turns into spiritual discourse. Those, who converse with Jangama, are saved forthwith. World that is passed by Jangama, gets purified. Spot visited by Jangama, becomes a pilgrimage. Water that is touched by Jangama, becomes holy water. And all those who pledge devotion to the

One, become the One.

Thus ends Prabhudeva's Sampadane auspiciously with vachana number seventy-eight.

Chapter 2

MUKTĀYAKKA'S SAMPĀDANE

The second chapter describes Prabhudēva's encounter with intensely grieving Muktāyakka over the death of her older brother Ajagaṇṇa who had lived in secret piety. Allama Prabhudeva shows her the way to achieve the Absolute – Shunya Sampadane.

At this juncture, it is to be pointed out to the readers that, although the Upanishads do not prescribe gender discrimination, some of the subsequent secondary scriptures, particularly the 'Manu Smriti' which is called the laws of Manu, stating that women cannot attain liberation on their own, held women in bondage for centuries in India. The honor of breaking this unjust law goes to the twelfth century Sharanas. **The Sharanas proclaimed 'Women, not just the men, can achieve liberation on their own'.** The attainment is within the reach of anyone whether it is a man or a woman, or of any caste or creed, and it is not a monopoly of a chosen few.

It is said that Muktāyakka's Sampadane exemplifies the Sharanas' view that women achieve liberation on their own, just as men do.

The first vachana in the second chapter tells of Muktāyakka's mourning her bereavement.

Vachana 1 on pages 148 and 149 in volume II of Shunya Sampadane (1) is as follows:

This mortal world holds Consciousness
Like a morsel pushed into a jaw.
It fails to swallow Consciousness
And hence is doomed to loss.
How can I survive O brother?
I have become as one who
Blinks between light and dark.
O Ajagaṇṇa, your yoga has first blindfolded my eyes, and then shown me the mirror!

Allama Prabhudeva encounters this grieving Muktāyakka, and consoles Muktāyakka who was undergoing the pangs of separation. Prabhudeva consoles her by assuring that Ajagaṇṇa, who had direct experience of the Divine, could never perish. **Ātman neither dies nor can it be killed.** To mourn him who is completely identified with the Absolute implies ignorance. When Ajagaṇṇa has attained the Absolute, there is no need to mourn as if he was just an ordinary individual.

Vachana 11 in chapter two of Shunya Sampadane is as follows:

Tell me, should you mourn for the self
Gone back to the 'Self', where
Neither consciousness nor yet oblivion is?

Tell me, should you grieve?

Look, the saying that
The destruction waits the disembodied soul,

Is wrong!

Lo! To him who has attained
The Ultimate Bliss,
There is neither one nor two,
Nor yet within and without,
And such is Guheshvara's Sharaṇa Ajagaṇṇa!

The above concept is in many Upanishads. It is described very well in Bhagavad-Gita (5).

After consoling the grieving Muktāyakka, Prabhudeva alleviates her anxiety of not having Ajagaṇṇa as her Guru.

Allama Prabhudeva makes a strong point that there is no necessity of an external Guru for the one who is well advanced in the path of self-realization. Vachana 24 on pages 175 and 176 in volume I of Shunya Sampadane (1) is something like this:

There is neither far, nor near between Guru and disciple!
It is the Guru's sport to be disciple, and
It is the disciple's sport to be the Guru.
May be there is a split, because this wretched karma has wedged between the two.
If you say you have become the self-effulgent light at the sight of the Absolute,
Who was ever was the created and incarnate farther back,
Then you are the Guru of yourself, superior to yourself.

Is there a need to tell that Guheshvara-Linga is none other than yourself?

There is no duality between the Guru and the disciple. One who knows one's Self, the Knowledge itself becomes the Guru. Here again, Prabhudeva is pointing out that **for those who are well advanced in their spiritual attainment, there is no need for an external physical Guru.**

Then he continues to teach her wisdom. If one identifies oneself with the body and mind, forgetting the inner self, the chain of worldly attachment will hold tight, and will be the cause of rebirth. One has to divest oneself from this attachment.

In this context, Prabhudēva states that one who has realized the Absolute cannot be characterized. Vachana 32 in chapter two of Shūnya Saṁpādane is as follows:

When the body's sheen is absorbed in the Liṅga,
The devotee is past the body's doubt.

When the lustre of breath is dissolved in consciousness,
The devotee needs not the traffic of words.

Moving, he moves not; speaking, he speaks not;
For Guheshvara's devotee no symbol needs!

When the luminous life-force is absorbed into the Conscious-force, all words and activity cease and there is no need for an external symbol.

Then there is this Prabhudēva's vachana which is somewhat enigmatic but profound in the sense that the **Absolute of the Veerashaivas has Consciousness**. Vachana 38 in chapter two of volume I of Shūnya Saṁpādane is as follows:

In speech, the action is consumed;
In action the speech is consumed.
Look, the traces of the will, of their own
Accord have gone to hide their shame!
Mark you, the consciousness of Guheshvara
Is sure an utterly barren thing.

This point that **the Absolute Shūnya of Theistic Monism Philosophy of the Veerashaivas is not only Self-luminous but also Self-conscious**, is important in order to differentiate it from the Absolute Brahman of Advaitism of Shankarāchārya (Absolute Monism Philosophy).

According to Shankarāchārya's Advaita Philosophy, all consciousness is activity, and activity limits the indeterminate Absolute Brahman, thus, Brahman is tranquil and is not Self-conscious – Brahman is Pure Knowledge, not Consciousness; Brahman is Self-luminous but not Self-Conscious.

Muktāyakka's vachana, vachana 41, is the last vachana in this second chapter. It is as follows:

Once you have attained the Absolute
Through contact with his Sharanas,
There is no knowing nor forgetting,
No union and no parting!

Having transcended the bounds of mind,
And tasted the joy of the Infinite,
Could you say, call it either
Shunya (Void) or Nisshunya (Primal Void)?

Once I am lost in my brother Ajagaṇṇa,
I have lost all speech, and have become
Camphor consumed in fire!

With Prabhudeva's Grace, a marvelous transformation takes place in Muktāyakka, and she realizes the Absolute.

There are 41 vachanas in this chapter. The subtotal comes to 119 vachanas.

Chapter 3

SIDDHARĀMAYYA'S SAMPĀDANE

This third chapter describes Prabhudēva's first encounter with Siddharāmayya. It seems that Siddharāmayya was mostly practicing Shaiva Philosophy which was not acceptable to Prabhudeva. There is an intense discussion of the Veerashaiva Philosophy between them. Prabhudeva teaches Siddharamayya, the concepts of Veerashaivism.

Siddharāmayya is known as Siddharāma of Sonnalige. Sonnalige is the present day city of Sholapur in the State of Maharashtra in India. Sometimes Siddharamayya is respectfully referred to as Siddharāmeshvara and also as the Great Shivayogi Siddharāma. Many relics - the Liṅgas he installed, the temples he built, water-tanks he constructed, and such - can be seen even to this present day.

The Legendary Story of Siddharamayya

A legendary story is given in the introduction part by the editors (1). It is as follows:

Siddharāmayya's parents were Muddagauḍa and Suggavve. It is said that one day, a while before Siddharamayya was born, Shree Rēvaṇasiddheshvara, a great Guru of that time, came to his parents' home and prophesized that they would be the parents of a great Yogi. That prophesy came true - Siddharamayya was later born endowed with splendid features.

When Siddharamayya was about 10 years of age, he was sent by his parents into the fields to graze the cattle every day. There, he routinely worshipped Shivaliṅga under a mango tree, and shared his food with his companions.

One day a Jangama by name Mallikārjuna of Shrishaila came before him. Siddharamayya being very pleased, offered his food to the Jangama who then wanted some buttermilk and gruel. Siddharamayya ran home and brought what the Jangama wanted. But, by that time, Jangama Mallikārjuna had disappeared. Siddharamayya was very disappointed, and started crying and sobbing 'Mallayya', 'Mallayya'. Some pilgrims who were on their way to the holy place Shrishaila, encountered this sobbing boy and offered him that they could take him to Shrishaila where they would show him Mallikārjuna. Accepting the offer, Siddharamayya went with the pilgrims. But he was again disappointed when the pilgrims showed him the Mallikārjuna Linga installed there in Shrishaila; he was expecting to see Jangama Mallikārjuna in person.

Siddharamayya was in despair. It is said that Divine Mallikārjuna appeared to Siddharamayya and told him to go home and take up some philanthropic work. Accordingly,

Siddharamayya went back to his place and was engaged in installing Sthāvara-Liṅgas (large stationary Liṅgas, usually inside temples), building temples and spires, constructing water-tanks, water sheds, alms sheds and such things. He also became an eminent Shivayogi and practiced 'Yoga and Shivayoga'.

Philosophical Discussion

While Siddharamayya was engaged in the pursuit of his philanthropic work, Prabhudeva arrives there in the course of his tour. Prabhudeva, after a long discussion with Siddharamayya, convinces that the deeds he was doing and the Yoga he was performing, will not help him achieve complete realization, and that he should concentrate on the inner discipline. Shunya Sampadane depicts this encounter with a detailed philosophical discussion in this third chapter.

All this discussion is in the vachanas.

Prabhudeva disapproves the temple building and temple worship. One of Prabhudeva's vachanas makes this clear. Vachana 4 on pages 220 and 221 in volume I of Shunya Sampadane (1) is like this:

When the body itself is the temple,
Why build a stone temple elsewhere?
When the breath itself has become Linga,
Why ask for a Linga elsewhere?
It is not for me to tell;

It is not for ears to hear.
O Guheshvara,
If you should turn into a stone,
What should I be?

If one builds a stone temple for a stone idol with the belief that God is stone and stone is God, then that Bhakta is no better than that stone. When the body itself is the temple of God, why build a stone temple elsewhere? When the life-breath itself has become Linga, why ask for a Linga elsewhere?

All works of charity, such as building water tanks for the benefit of all, building alms sheds and giving food to the poor, and speaking the truth, is well and good; it will only take the person, after death, to heaven to be reborn after the exhaustion of the fruits of good deeds. It will not lead to full realization and liberation from the cycle of births and deaths.

Siddharamayya was an accomplished Yogi in all aspects. Shunya Sampadane extolls Siddharamayya in this regard. The Yoga he was performing has been mentioned as *'Yoga and Shivayoga'.* In one of the vachanas of Siddharamayya, *'Karma Yoga'* is mentioned. Prabhudeva, in his vachana, uses the term *'karmakāṇḍa-yoga'* for the 'Yoga and Shivayoga' that Siddharamayya was performing. Karmakāṇḍa refers to the first part or the ritualistic part of the Vedas; this part of the Veda is shunned by the Veerashaivas.

The main part of the Shunya Sampadane itself does not mention the term *'Kundalini-Yoga'* anywhere in it. The editors of volume I of Shunya Sampadane (1), mention Kundalini-Yoga in the explanatory notes section of the book to explain some of the components of the 'Yoga and Shivayoga' which were being performed by the great Shivayogi Siddharāma. It is to be pointed out to the readers that the Veerashaivas do not perform the Kundalini Yoga of the Tantra system.

There is an extensive and intense discussion of Siddharāmayya's way of performing 'Yoga and Shivayoga'. Prabhudeva disapproves Siddharāmayya's way, and helps him see the right Veerashaiva way.

While Siddharamayya was singing the praise, Prabhudeva, mocking at the praise, tells Siddharamayya that the 'One' who has neither form nor body nor motion and who is beyond the reach of word or thought, cannot be attained by praise - for the 'One' transcends praise and scorn alike.

Vachana 43 on pages 257 and 258 in volume I of Shunya Sampadane (1) is as follows:

You cannot grasp Him, as you can
Those who have donned the body.
He does not move this way and that,
As breathing mortals do.
You cannot size Him up with eyes,
Nor measure Him with ears.

Look you, O Siddharamayya
Guheshvara's glory
Cannot be grasped by simple flattery!

In response, Siddharamayya describes progressive modes of worship where praise is involved – simple praise of God, concentration on the image of God, efforts to apprehend the real nature of God, and the constant harboring of God in the heart. Siddharamayya declares that all these stages of devotion to God are God's own gifts.

But, Prabhudeva responds by saying that those who try to realize God by offering hymns of praise remain confined to the personal aspect of God that they describe in their hymns. God is not fond of praise or prayer, but is fond of true-devotion and real love. Several paths cannot attain to Him by hymns of praise; lip homage without works is not the way to the goal. **Rituals and rites cannot escape rebirth.**

Prabhudeva compassionately extolls Siddharāmayya's achievement as the great Yogi and Shivayogi, and says that Siddharamayya has attained realization in the Brahmarandhra (conceptualized to be at the top of the brain/head). But, Siddharamayya responds by saying that he does not know all Yoga's ways; it is not Yoga if there is no union of Shiva-Shakti; with Shiva-Shakti apart, there is no Yoga, and if the 'One' is not serene within the lotus of the heart, there is no freedom.

Prabhudeva comments: The wise are able to control their desires and cravings by their own will-power; they are self-dependent. Whereas, the devout rely on God to help them in their spiritual discipline; they are dependent on other's aid. But, there are some others who are more advanced than either of the above two. They transcend the difference between Jnana and Bhakti; they are the true Veerashaiva Sharanas.

Siddharamayya presents his devotional service to Prabhudeva; it is described in Yogic terminology. Then he requests Prabhudeva to instruct him out of his kindness. Prabhudeva, however, says that mere exposition of the nature of the Absolute by others does not enable one to realize it. **One has to realize it by self-effort, like meditation and concentration.** Once one has found the secret of the union of the body and soul, one will discover one's own true identity. The presumption that knowledge is impossible to attain implies ignorance; so long as this persists, the knowledge of the Self is not attained. **The all-pervading Absolute cannot be sought anywhere outside.** The aspirant's persistent longing to see the Absolute and realize it is always associated with eagerness and urgency; it precludes the aspirant from knowing oneself. When the aspirant has known oneself, the longing to know the Absolute ceases.

Prabhudeva asks Siddharamayya why he has become the object of his own desire and the goal of his own search, and why should a temple be built apart for the sake of a devotee.

Siddharamayya responds by saying that he undertook to build the temples in the imitation of the Lord Himself who created innumerable creatures; each temple containing the Lord's image, an atom containing an atom.

Veerashaivas do not worship an 'image' of God; they worship God itself.

Prabhudeva counters that it is wrong to assume that all the creatures of the world can be regarded as temples, and that his assumption that he has brought the Linga from the farthest zone, meaning from the Sahasrāra (also called Brahmarandhra at the top of the head), to the central zone, meaning to the heart, is a mere boast.

Siddharamayya submits that whatever he does is all under the governance of the Lord, and that he has no freedom apart from the Lord, and requests Prabhudeva to make him realize himself.

Prabhudeva, in his vachana, uses the term *'karmakāṇḍa-yoga'* for the 'Yoga and Shivayoga' that Siddharamayya was performing (Karmakāṇḍa refers to the first part or the ritualistic part of the Vedas; this part of the Veda is shunned by the Veerashaivas), and says that temples and tanks are the footprints of the past; rituals and rites cannot escape rebirth; one has to shatter the ties of yesterday and tomorrow, and bind fast to the

Absolute.

Siddharamayya, then, presents his Yoga as a process where one stage follows another, and says that it is necessary that one must do some action in order to gain knowledge. Here, Siddharāmayya's Kannada vachana uses the term '*Karma-Yoga*'. Karma-Yoga is very well described in Bhagavad-Gita (5).

Prabhudeva responds by saying that this type of empirical knowledge does not put one into direct contact with the Reality. **Acquisition of knowledge is through intuition.** The empirical knowledge is to be transcended if one would know the Reality through mystic experience.

In order to reach the highest state, one must transcend the three Linga divisions.

Vachana 97 on page 313 in volume I of Shunya Sampadane (1) is as follows:

The Jyotir-Linga in the eyes,
The Ubhayapratishtheya-Linga on the palm,
The Amrita-Linga in the Brahmarandhra:
The apartness of these three must be destroyed, O Siddharamayya,
If you would know Guheshvara-Linga.

Siddharamayya says that through his Yoga he has cleaned his mind with water of peace and mercy, and has gotten rid of the passions. And then, focusing his mind to a single point, has completed the gradual process of its purification. Here, the 'water of peace and mercy' may refer to the *'Pādōdaka'.* Padodaka is the water that has washed the feet of Guru and Jangama. Padodaka is also the water that has washed the Ishtalinga. It is to be pointed out that the Sharanas are more interested in the symbolic meaning of Padodaka than its literal meaning. Symbolically, Padodaka is Bliss *(Ānanda).* It is implied that Padodaka is the enlightenment of Supreme-Bliss that flows like water from Guru, Linga and Jangama to the disciple.

Prabhudeva asks *'What Yoga is this to wash the mind and make it clean?'*

Siddharamayya, then describes his Yoga experience as follows:

- Through discernment, the movement of the nine energy-conduits/channels is stayed;
- Through it the central channel (Sushumna) is purified;
- Through it the eight-petal-lotus is turned upwards and made to stand in its right position;
- Through it the fifty-two letters (of the Kannada alphabet) are scanned and concentrated in a single one.
- All this has been accomplished through the power of thought.

And then, Siddharamayya continues, he has climbed to the summit of the path that leads along the central channel Sushumna, and have enthroned the Divine in the thousand-petal-lotus Sahasrāra at the top of the head/brain (also known as Brahmarandhra).

The central channel Sushumna of the Vedas goes from the heart to the top of the head. It is an energy channel/conduit (nāḍi or nāḷa). Whereas the Sushumna of the Tantra system goes from the base chakra that is said to be located at the level of the lower end of the vertebral column (tip of the coccyx), to the top of the head to the Sahasrāra/Brahmarandhra.

Prabhudeva analyzes the Yoga practiced by Siddharamayya and says that the type of Yoga he is practicing is not acceptable. The analysis is as follows:

- It is not Yoga to say one knows the subtle way the nine channels move;
- It is not Yoga to say one has been able to scan the fifty-two characters and have been caught within the lotus of the heart;
- If one says the Absolute is within, then the Absolute must be quite inert;
- If one says the Absolute is without, then It is beyond the range of mind and speech;
- The Absolute is not above the six wheels or lotuses.

Prabhudeva condemns the performance of what appears to be the Kundalini type of Yoga.

Prabhudeva continues:

- It is an immeasurable loss for those who say that they have sat in the comfortable lotus pose, broken the rigor of the spinal-cord, opened a path behind with the aid of faith, and have eaten the nectar of immortality.
- When you see what the Veda says that *'He is past ten-finger measurement'* (this comes in the Purusha-sukta of Rigveda X.90.1), you cannot establish Him by touch.
- When the Absolute is beyond such words as to signify position and measurement, you cannot see Him in Brahmarandhra.
- Listen Siddharamayya, Guheshvara-Linga (The Absolute Divine) transcends imagination's reach!

Siddharamayya: I do not think of Him as form, nor do I loose myself in thought of Him. I do not set Him up somewhere beyond our ten-finger measurement and remain myself elsewhere.

Siddharamayya continues: I have made myself the base called Omkāra (Om-form), have enthroned on it the Linga called the Silent-One, and, attaining to in-separate union, have made Om into form.

Prabhudeva: If Nada (which refers to unstruck sound/vibration) is to be the Linga, and Bindu (which refers to a dot, a point or a drop) its base as you say, then that is a divided Linga. Only when their pure conjunction called Kala (art of creating) is effected, that it transcends Nada, Bindu and Kala.

Prabhudeva continues: Identification (aikya) with the Supreme Linga will not bear thought of here and there. **To say the Supreme Linga is an embodiment of Om-form is wrong. Om form is Shabda-Brahman (shabda means sound), whereas the Absolute is 'Silence'.**

Siddharamayya: When I said Nada and Bindu, I only meant the affinity of Anga and Linga. Because, Nada has become life, and Bindu has become the body, both of them are free from all impurity. Only those who have realized the union of Nada and Bindu know the nature of the absorbed mind.

Prabhudeva explains:

- The will is not free from the instinctive urges while the mind is still attached to the unconscious. Spiritual evolution consists in the development of the pure and conscious will, and its ultimate emancipation from the unconscious. Ignorance with its doubts and desires should be overcome by acquiring knowledge. Then the aspirant is expected to eliminate even the awareness of having dispelled the ignorance.
- Excessive concern to transcend the will is itself servitude to will. If you talk of merging the mind in Him, it only proves that the mind exists.
- Shivayogi does not speak of merging his mind in Parashiva, because, his mind has already been merged; Shivayogi by definition has no separate mind.

Siddharamayya: Where is the fallacy if I refer to mind-absorbing Yoga? What is so wonderful in speaking of Brahman without mind and utterly void? Is there a difference in the spoken word and its meaning?

Prabhudeva: One cannot talk of mind after the mind has merged in the Absolute.

Siddharamayya: Once there is identity between Anga and Linga, the body, mind and words have all been divinized; there should be no clash of words.

Prabhudeva gives three illustrations to explain it further:

- When a heap of camphor burns, there is no charcoal to be found.
- When the sun shines at its pinnacle, there is no mist.
- When a waxen dart is shot into a pile of burning coal, the waxen dart is not found again.
- **When you have known the Absolute, you will not speak for it as God.** (Once you have become the Absolute Shūnya itself, then there is nothing else – no God, no devotee, and nothing.)

Siddharamayya: When I have known the consciousness embracing the thought of having lost myself, how could I forget what I have known?

Prabhudeva describes the nature of the

Trance of the Absolute void as a statement on the oneness philosophy:

- When one says, one has known, one has forgotten, or one has known and forgotten, all that is the Absolute. To say that It is in the very thought that forgets the outward sign of consciousness is also the Absolute.
- When the mind is lost in the Highest beyond space, when the Highest is lost in mind released from brain, when all tremor has been stilled, there is no room for more. It is like camphor lost in fire.

Siddharamayya, being pleased and grateful with Prabhudeva's explanation of the Sharana Philosophy, says that, because of his acts of temple building and such, Prabhudeva came there and dispelled his ignorance. Siddharamayya then requests Prabhudeva to explain the way of experiencing the undivided Linga with the aid of the symbol Ishtalinga. (Please note that Siddharamayya was not wearing Ishtalinga at that time.)

Prabhudeva explains the principle of 'annihilating the symbol through symbol'. It is something like this:

- The difference between Ishṭaliṅga and Prāṇaliṅga is that the word 'without' appears before the word 'within'.
- Liṅga consciousness possessing mind should not have any un-tranquil thought during

this process.

- **Focusing both mind and will, both thought and sight on the Liṅga enthroned on the palm with the unwinking gaze and losing all consciousness of 'in' and 'out', one experiences the undivided Liṅga.** (That is how one experiences the undivided Liṅga with the aid of the symbol Ishṭaliṅga.)

Then Prabhudeva says that Basavanna has realized the entire experience, and that they should get everything explained by him at the city of Kalyana. They both go to Kalyana together.

This third chapter has 140 vachanas. The subtotal so far comes to 259 vachanas.

The above three chapters are in volume I of the referenced Shūnya Saṁpādane (1). The second volume starts with the fourth chapter.

Chapter 4

THE SAMPĀDANE CONCERNING THE GRACE BESTOWED BY BASAVAṆṆA UPON CHENNABASAVAṆṆA

In this fourth chapter, in the prose section, the **glory of Basavaṇṇa** is given first. Some of the descriptions of the glory of Basavanna are as follows: He is the gross principle of Parashiva; restorer of the practice of Veerashaivism which had been tarnished by the six Darshanas (Darshanas are the six Schools of Philosophy, namely, *Sāṁkhya, Nyāya, Vaishēshika, Yoga, Pūrva Mīmāmsa,* and *Uttara Mīmāmsa*) and six Samayas (Samayas are the six creeds belonging to the Tantra system, namely, *Shaiva, Shakta, Vaishnava, Gāṇāpatya, Soura,* and *Kāpālika*); practiced in the city of Kalyana worshipping Guru Linga and Jangama; and many such adorations.

It is also stated there that **Basavaṇṇa lived happily fostering the true Veerashaiva faith.**

The editors of volume II of the referenced Shunya Sampadane (1), give the following information about Basavanna.

Basavaṇṇa

Basava, popularly known as Basavaṇṇa and respectfully known as Basaveshvara, was born into a respectable and cultured family in the year 1131 or 1132 CE (AD) at Bāgevāḍi in the Bijapur district of Karnāṭaka. The parents were Mādarasa and Mādalāmbike. However, some historians opine that Basavaṇṇa was born in the village of Ingaleshvara the place of his maternal grand-parents. In India at that time it was customary for the full-term pregnant woman to go to her parents place for the maternity care. It is possible that that is what happened, and thus Basavanna was born there.

Both the parents were extremely pious and devoted to religious vows and practices. It is said that they belonged to a Brahmin sect. These Brahmins are also called Ārādhyas. They are the Veerashaiva Brahmins who practice Brahminical rites and rituals including the varṇāshrama duties. The Veerashaiva Brahmins are worshippers of Personal Liṅga (Ishṭaliṅga).

Nāgamma who was also known as Nāgalāmbike and Akkanāgamma, was Basavaṇṇa's elder sister by about 12 years. They were the only two children for their parents. Basavaṇṇa grew up in the company of his sister who is said to have influenced his revolutionary ideas.

When Basavaṇṇa was about eight years old, as per the religious tradition, his father Mādarasa performed Upanayana (religious thread ceremony). Basavaṇṇa revolted against the ritualistic religious ceremonies, and he left his home and came to the holy place Kūḍala Saṅgama which is also called Kappaḍi Saṅgama.

Basavaṇṇa's parents could not convince him to return, therefore they requested Nāgalāmbike to take care of her brother there at Kūḍala Saṅgama. Nāgalāmbike had already married to her husband Shivasvāmi at the time. According to her parents' request, Nāgalāmbike moved to Kūḍala Saṅgama from her and her husband's place Ingaleshvara along with her husband Shivasvāmi.

The holy place Kūḍala Saṅgama is located about 35 miles south-southwest of Basavana Bāgevāḍi at the confluence of Krishna and Malaprabha Rivers.

Saṅgamanātha/Saṅgamēshvara Temple complex is located there at Kūḍala Saṅgama. There, there was then a learned scholar Īshānya Guru, under whom Basavaṇṇa studied the Vedas, Āgamas, Shāstras, and other sacred religious literature. Basavaṇṇa was there for about ten years and learned everything from his Guru Īshānya. Basavaṇṇa's day to day worship of Lord Kūḍala Saṅgama, at the site, brought him peace of mind and spiritual fulfillment.

Harihara, a very well-known and distinguished Kannaḍa writer, the author of 'Basavarājadēvara Ragaḷe', implies that the Divine Kūḍala Saṅgamanātha himself came to Basavaṇṇa, and commanded him to leave Kūḍala

Saṅgama for the good of all. Basavaṇṇa was content in staying put at Kūḍala Saṅgama, but, Saṅgamanātha assured Basavaṇṇa that he would always be with him, and came to Basavaṇṇa's palm in the form of Ishṭaliṅga through Nandikeshvara. This incident has been said to represent Basavaṇṇa's **Liṅga initiation**. But, the editors of volume II of the referenced Shūnya Saṁpādane (1), on page four of volume II, state as follows: 'Accounts differ regarding the time and the place of the initiation of Basavaṇṇa. According to Siṅgirāja (Siṅgirāja Purāṇa chapter V.54-61, pp. 67-68) it was performed by Jatavedamuni at Bāgevāḍi soon after the birth of Basavaṇṇa. Bhimakavi (Basava Purāṇa Ch. III.24-29, pp. 40-41) agrees with Siṅgirāja regarding the time and place of the ceremony, but says that it was Saṅgamēshvara Himself who performed the rite'. The editor of the referenced Siddhānta Shikhāmaṇi (6), gives this information in the note section on page 378: Basavaṇṇa obtained his Veerashaiva initiation from Shrī Jātaveda muni (Saṅgamēshvara Svāmīji) of Sāraṅgmath at Kūḍala Saṅgama.

The biographers differ on **whom Basavaṇṇa married.** It is said that Basavaṇṇa had two wives – the first wife Gaṅgādevi or Gaṅgāmbike, and the second wife Māyidevi. Gaṅgāmbike was the daughter of Basavaṇṇa's maternal uncle Baladeva who was King Bijjaḷa's minister (1). According to Siṅgirāja, (Siṅgirāja Purāṇa Ch. VII.53. p. 107), he married

Nīlalōchane, the King Bijjaḷa's foster-sister. Shūnya Saṁpādane (1) itself, at the end, in its twenty-first chapter, portrays Nīlalōchane as Basavaṇṇa's wife (see below in this article), and does not say anything about whether she was King Bijjaḷa's foster sister or not. Also, Shūnya Saṁpādane itself does not mention anything about Gaṅgādevi and Māyidevi. It seems that Māyidevi is Nīlalōchane who was king Bijjaḷa's foster sister, and Basavaṇṇa married both Gaṅgāmbike and Nīlalōchane.

Basavaṇṇa started as a clerk in king Bijjaḷa's court, and then **worked** as the head of the treasury. He later became the Prime Minister. King Bijjaḷa ruled from the capital city of Kalyāṇa over a large territory of the present day Karnāṭaka, Andhra Pradesh, and Maharashtra states in India.

Most of Basavaṇṇa's adult life and his work were at Kalyāṇa. **The city of Kalyāṇa** was the site of a great religious movement in the 12th century that led to the revitalization and reformation of the then existing Veerashaiva, Shaiva and other sects of the Hindu religion.

Basavaṇṇa initiated a movement to reform Veerashaivism from within. His efforts were mostly oriented in two directions – religion and society (1).

He saw no difference between rich and poor, and between man and woman; he saw no difference among different castes; and he embedded this principle of equality among all, in the religion. He insisted upon the dignity and necessity of manual work; all work was equal in his eyes and in the eyes of God. The work was dedicated work (kāyaka) in the form of worship. Furthermore, surrendering all the fruits of one's labor for the welfare of humanity (dāsōha) was one of the essential tenets of his faith. (1).

The reforms were rooted in profound humility. He did not, on his own, want to lay down the law in matters of religion and philosophy. Therefore, **he founded the Anubhava Maṇṭapa** where a large number of philosophers, mystics, scholars and seekers would gather to participate in learned discussions on the philosophical aspects of religious life. They came from all parts of the Indian subcontinent. Kalyāṇa was both a symbol and an actual place where the Anubhava Maṇṭapa became a spiritual academy. (1).

A new Philosophical System was developed and practical implementation of the ideas was carried out. This did not go well with the traditionalists in King Bijjaḷa's court.

The event that precipitated a violent action by Bijjaḷa was that of the so called inter-caste marriage. The parents of the bride and the groom had already embraced the Veerashaiva faith. Therefore, technically it was not an inter-caste marriage. Anyway, Madhuvarasa, the father of the bride was of the Brahmin caste, and Haraḷayya, the father of the groom was a cobbler.

King Bijjaḷa was kind of forced by traditionalists in his kingdom to take such violent action where both the fathers of the bride and groom were cruelly executed. Basavaṇṇa sensing a violent reaction from among his more headlong followers, pacified them. He then resigned from his position as the Prime-minister to King Bijjaḷa, and hurriedly left Kalyāṇa and went to Kūḍala Saṅgama.

Gūḷūra Siddhavīraṇārya, the composer of the referenced fourth version of Shūnya Saṁpādane (1) makes **a point in dispute:** On page 406 of volume V, it is stated in the prose section that Basavaṇṇa gave orders to Jagadeva to proclaim the truth by slaying Bijjaḷa the ill-wisher of the devotees of Shiva. And then on the same page gives Basavaṇṇa's vachana which states 'Bijjaḷa must die at Jagadeva and Molleya Bommaṇṇa's hand'.

However, first it is to be pointed out that the same Basavaṇṇa's vachana is in the Gaṇaka Vachana Saṁpuṭa reference (3), but there, this vachana 625 does not include that type of statement.

Furthermore, the editors of volume V of the referenced fourth version of Shūnya Saṁpādane (1) in the introduction part on page 378 of volume V, state - 'This is not in perfect conformity with the facts of history as have since come to light', and refer to pages 7 and 8 in volume II of Shūnya Saṁpādane for the explanation. It is stated there that some writings claim that Basavaṇṇa himself was directly or indirectly responsible for the death of Bijjaḷa, and that even Shūnya Saṁpādane seems to accept this view, but the two prose passages in the fourth version of Shūnya Saṁpādane were a later addition, and that this type of account of what happened is not found in the first two older versions of Shūnya Saṁpādane compiled by Shivagaṇaprasādi Mahādēvayya and by Halageyadēva.

Then the editors say that Siṅgirāja, the author of Siṅgirāja Purāṇa, relates how Basavaṇṇa pacified his followers and averted the danger to Bijjaḷa's life. At the time of assassination of Bijjaḷa, Basavaṇṇa had already left Kalyāṇa. More than all this, there is the entire personality of Basavaṇṇa as revealed by his own vachanas and in those of his contemporaries as well as of his immediate successors, which indicate that Basavaṇṇa was incapable of any type of violent action, let alone a murder.

Basavaṇṇa upon receiving farewell from innumerable saints sent them away, and he went towards Kappaḍi (Kūḍala Saṅgama or simply Kūḍali). King Bijjaḷa got killed. Basavaṇṇa, after reaching Kūḍali, sent Haḍapada Appaṇṇa to bring his wife Nīlalōchane to Kūḍali. But Nīlalōchane did not want to go there. She states 'it does not matter whether I am here or there; through attainment of the Absolute, I enjoy the ultimate bliss, and there is no separation between Basavaṇṇa and me'. Appaṇṇa comes back to Kūḍali and reports Nīlalōchane's decision not to come there to Basavaṇṇa, who accepts the news.

Basavaṇṇa's return to Kūḍala Saṅgama was in 1167 CE. He spends **his final days** there. Basavaṇṇa continuing his intense internal worship and meditation remarks that the Sharaṇa is ready for the Union (Aikya) and that he does not want any other place in the body of Kūḍala Saṅgama Dēva but only on the one seat throne in the innermost core of the heart lotus. At that juncture, because Basavaṇṇa had gotten Prabhudēva's merciful grace, the Liṅga of the Higher Consciousness appears in splendor to Basavaṇṇa at the center of his innermost mind. As when the lightening issues from a cloud like a clustered mass of light of a billion suns, taking a form of concentrated light of a billion moons, Saṅgamēshvara comes in the form of a Jaṅgama, and embracing Basavaṇṇa and so absorbing him in the lotus of his heart, draws Basavaṇṇa into Liṅga. It is said that, at that moment, Shivabhaktas' songs everywhere resounded with acclamation.

Saṅgamanātha/Saṅgamēshvara Temple complex is located at Kūḍala Saṅgama. More importantly, the Basaveshvara Aikya Maṇṭapa and Aikyaliṅga are located there. Newer developments – Gateway, Basavaṇṇa's statue in a worshipping position, Basava Dharma Pita, Sabha Mandira (Auditorium), and Basava International Center –

are of interest also. The site is fairly well developed for visitors. It is a vast area and not within any urban town. Accommodation is available – with air-conditioned and non-air-conditioned rooms, and a restaurant service. (This part of the information is as of January 2010.)

Basavaṇṇa's birthday known as **Basava Jayanti** is celebrated every year by the Liṅgāyatas/Veerashaivas and also by some of the Shaivas and other Hindus. His birthday is said to be on the third day of the first bright half of the second month Vaiśākha of the Hindu Lunar Calendar. The twelve months of the Lunar year come to 354 days only, whereas the Solar year has 365.25 days. Although the Lunar year usually consists of 12 months, in order to equalize the Lunar and Solar years, sometimes the Lunar year may have 11 or 13 months. The details aside, the point is that, Basava Jayanti falls on different dates every year on the solar calendar. The third day in the first bright half of the month of Vaiśākha of the Hindu Lunar Calendar, in the solar year 2021, was on Friday May 14. In the solar year 2022, Basava Jayanti is on Tuesday May 3. However, in North America, Basavaṇṇa's birthday is celebrated on a convenient day in the month of May or June, or even in the month of July.

Basavaṇṇa's vachanas seem to be somewhat more popular than those of his contemporary authors. There does not seem to be any dispute about the number of vachanas of

Basavaṇṇa that are available now. Reference (3) has all 1426 vachanas of Basavaṇṇa in Kannaḍa, and it also has English translations of most of the vachanas.

Grace bestowed by Basavaṇṇa upon Chennabasavaṇṇa

A brief biography of Chennabasavanna is given in chapter eight under Chennabasavanna's Sampadane to come later in this book.

Chennabasavanna was Basavanna's nephew. He was the son of Basavanna's elder sister Akkanāgamma. Basavanna had bestowed initiation (Lingadhāraṇa) upon Chennabasavanna while Akkanāgamma was eight-months pregnant with him.

It is stated there in the prose section that Chennabasavaṇṇa was the cause for the Shaṭsthala doctrine being expounded to all the Saints, and that he was responsible for the coming of Allama Prabhudēva to Kalyāṇa. The editors of volume II of the referenced Shūnya Saṁpādane (1), in the notes and comments section state that it is Chennabasavaṇṇa who systematized the Shaṭsthala philosophy, drawing mainly on the knowledge and mystic experience of the contemporary Sharaṇas.

In this chapter, Shūnya Saṁpādane tries to depict the difference between Liṅgadhāraṇe and Dīkshā. Chennabasavaṇṇa already had his

Liṅgadhāraṇe while he was still enwombed during his mother's pregnancy. Chennabasavaṇṇa calls this Liṅgadhāraṇe initiation as *'Sujñāna Upadēśa'.*

The significance of performing the initiation ceremony upon the enwombed child is that the unborn child at the 8th month stage becomes fully conscious of its divine nature, and is said to have the desire to break the fetters of bondage so as to attain spiritual liberation from the cycle of births and deaths.

The editors of volume II of the referenced Shunya Sampadane (1) give Garbhopanishad passage 4 as a reference. It is a minor Upanishad, and it states that the enwombed embryo cognizes in the ninth month etc. (15).

This belief, that the enwombed child at the 8th month stage can become fully cognizant of its divine nature, seems to have been based on the story of enwombed sage Vāmadeva given in Rigveda and the Aitareya Upanishad. The Aitareya Upanishad is one of the major Upanishads. The Aitareya Upanishad has this following passage in its second chapter. The translation is taken, as is, from the referenced Aitareya Upanishad book (22):

'Referring to the Highest Reality, there is the following Vedic verse (Rigveda IV.27.1) seen by the sage Vāmadeva: "Ah! Dwelling inside the womb I understood all the births of all the gods. A hundred bodies as strong as steel restrained me, but like a hawk I broke them by force and came

out swiftly". While yet in the womb Vāmadeva declared thus. Emerging thus from the body, enlightened with this supreme knowledge, and having enjoyed all delights in the abode of bliss he became immortal, verily he became immortal.'

Anyway, in one of his vachanas, Chennabasavanna tells Basavanna – *'the very day your fingers smeared the ashen mark upon me still enwombed, I had my blessing'.*

It seems that the above act by Basavaṇṇa while Chennabasavaṇṇa was still enwombed during his mother's pregnancy, meant for him that he had been blessed by Basavaṇṇa then.

Apparently, this did not seem to be enough for Chennabasavanna; he wanted Basavanna to bestow grace *(Dīkshā)* upon him at the stage when he had already been far advanced in his spirituality.

Upon Chennabasavanna's request, Basavanna was perplexed at the prospect of serving as a Guru to him who had already made great advances in the path of self-realization. Therefore, Basavanna refuses to do the honor.

This Basavanna's vachana, vachana 2 on pages 28 and 29 in volume II of Shunya Sampadane (1) is as follows:

Ho! Ho! What am I that should give instructions to anyone?

The men who were saved of old,

Did save themselves,
And all of them are one with Reality.
I had nothing to do with it.
To those who have held fast the truth,
I shall minister.
O Chennabasavanna,
Bear all the Immortals witness
Before Kudala Sangama Deva,
It is not for me to give
Grace that is rendered in words.

In the past the great ones saved themselves and attained Oneness with the True-Linga on their own. Basavanna did not have anything to do with them and they did not need an external Guru. Basavanna also says that he does not want to give the Grace that is rendered in words.

Chennabasavanna says that he is not going to give up obtaining instruction through Basavanna's grace. The principle of Guru-disciple relationship has been already established while enwombed, and the Guru-disciple principle is eternal.

Basavanna again declines and says that he sees Chennabasavanna as an embodiment of the Absolute because he wears the Linga on his body, and that the Linga is Lord Sangama Himself.

Chennabasavanna insists: 'You have already acted as a Guru and have blessed me with the Linga. How is it possible that you are saying I cannot do it in the deed? If you give your grace to me, I will make the great ones of the mortal world applaud me and vindicate you'.

Basavanna: *'Because you are so advanced and you are my Master, I can say neither yes nor no'.*

With that, Chennabasavanna places his Ishtalinga on the hands of Basavanna and asks him to mark its feature. But Basavanna instantly returns it and states that one should never seek features in the Linga. All the same, Chennabasavanna accepts that brief interaction itself as Divine Grace, and shouts with triumphal joy.

It is said in the prose section that Chennabasavaṇṇa having received his blessings from Basavaṇṇa, has achieved harmony between his inward knowledge and his outward actions, and is now endowed with all the disciplines and become fully accomplished. And that the initiation has bestowed upon him the peace of mind and certitude.

It is also said that Chennabasavaṇṇa does obeisance with extreme delight to Basavaṇṇa and praises him.

Basavaṇṇa thereupon, exceedingly pleased, mentions that becoming one with the Divine is like river merging in river and becoming one. Vachana 30 on pages 65 and 66 of volume II is as follows:

O Sir, what is the benefit of worshipping Liṅga,
Unless you have common love and common art?
O Sir, what is the benefit of worshipping Liṅga,
Unless you become one with Kūḍala Saṅgama Dēva,
Like river merging in river to become one?

After that, the arrival of Prabhudeva and Siddharamayya at the city of Kalyana, and the glory of the city of Kalyana are described. It is said in the prose section that there was a stone inscription in the form of Chennabasavaṇṇa's vachana about the glory of Kalyāṇa, installed at its gate. The vachana is given there in Shūnya Sampādane.

Then there is a glorious description of the Maṭha, the court-yard, and Basavaṇṇa's house.

There are 43 vachanas in this fourth chapter; subtotal so far is 302 vachanas.

Chapter 5

SAMPĀDANE DEALING WITH PRABHUDĒVA'S ARRIVAL AT THE CITY OF KALYĀṆA

Pre-eminence of Jangama over the Ishtalinga has been very well depicted in this fifth chapter. It is about the interaction between Bhakta Basavanna and Jangama Prabhudeva at their first encounter.

At the end of chapter 3 it has been stated that both Prabhudeva and Siddharamayya go to Kalyana together. Chapter five picks-up the story after they arrive at Kalyana.

Prabhudeva and Siddharamayya arrive at Basavanna's place in Kalyana. An assistant to Basavanna named Haḍapada Appaṇṇa who carries betel-nuts and leaves and such things for Basavanna and other Sharanas, upon seeing their arrival, not knowing their identity and awe struck with wonder by the personality of the one in Jangama guise (Allama Prabhudeva), joyfully goes and informs Basavanna of their arrival.

As Basavanna was deeply engrossed in Linga worship at the time, he asks Appaṇṇa to go and invite them in. Appaṇṇa goes and invites them.

But Prabhudeva resents that a messenger is sent to receive them instead of Basavanna coming himself, and wonders how such a Bhakta as Basavanna could falter in the path of devotion.

Bhakta should always be awake to the idea that pride is never compatible with Bhakti.

Prabhudeva remarks that he would not step into the house of such a one who, speaking advaita lore (monism doctrine), is obsessed with action, and shows no spirit of service.

Service to Jangama is more important than Ishtalinga-worship.

Appaṇṇa goes back to Basavanna and informs him of the refusal of the Jangama to step into the house.

Basavanna tells Appaṇṇa: 'Jangama wears the Bhakta's body, and Bhakta wears Jaṅgama's breath. They are inseparable. Bhakta and Jangama abide in both Bhakta and Jangama. To be a Jangama, you need bhakti. Jangama is one who enters the Bhakta's house as master claiming to be the lord of all Bhakta's riches, life and honor, and accepts all that Bhakta has and sanctifies. There is no need for Jangama to fret, because, it is like coming to one's own house. Bhakta, a mere keeper of the door of Sharanas' house, says neither yes nor no'.

Appaṇṇa goes back to the Jangama and conveys the message.

Prabhudeva then responds in his vachana:

- 'Who knows the link between Bhakta and Jangama? He is not a Bhakta simply because he has surrendered wealth breath and honor. He does not fit into the proper conduct in the spirit of truth'.
- 'He is not a Jangama who enters a Bhakta's house accepting his prostrations, eating food to satisfy his appetite, demanding money to gratify his vices, walking away with praise for those who give, and blame those who do not'.
- 'He is a Bhakta who having discerned and known the Absolute that is before time or of timelessness, who loosened and threw away the seam that knits the body and soul, and who is content to dedicate All-self to That'.
- 'He is a Jangama in whom there is no taint of fret or fervor, in whom there is no desire to gratify the body, in whom awareness has become his body, and in whom fulfilment is a form devotion takes'.
- 'Meeting of such a Jangama and such a Bhakta is a meeting indeed. The league and fellowship of others, the half-hearted Bhaktas, fails to please Guheshvara-Linga'.

Appaṇṇa, hearing this, comes back to Basavanna and says 'I am no Bhakta; he will not come in at my request; you go and fetch him graciously in'.

By then, Chennabasavanna, Basavanna's nephew, comes to Basavanna and says something like this in his vachana:

'If you cannot see the magnitude of your visiting Sharanas, then what price is the faith that held that all things wearing the Linga are Saṅgamanātha?

When Shiva has come in body, one should make haste and bow Sir!

When Prabhudeva and Siddharamayya, Shiva's Sharanas, have come and stand at your door, even if your eyes were shut from view, your heart should perceive that.

It is not proper for you to be casual and heedless to send a messenger, go yourself and fetch them graciously in'.

Basavanna, now trembling with fear, vented his utter despair: 'Behold, not having welcome them when Linga as Jangama came walking to my house, I feel all spiritless!' And then, with exceeding fear, begs Chennabasavanna to go appease Prabhudeva's anger and bring them in.

Chennabasavanna reiterates that Basavanna himself has to personally invite them, and states that Prabhudeva has come to test his heart and has screened his mind in sport.

Then, while Basavanna was consoling himself, Soḍḍaḷa Bācharasa, an elder prominent Sharana of the time, comes and also says that

Prabhudeva has set up a show to test Basavanna's heart, therefore, Basavanna need not fear, he just has to go and personally invite them in.

Basavanna continues to console himself, and realizing his mistake, ends his Ishtalinga worship, and states: *One worships Linga so that a Jangama should come to one's house; when the Jangama comes, the Linga worship stops and the Jangama worship begins; this is because, between Linga and Jangama, Jangama is pre-eminent.*

Vachana 20 on pages 143 and 144 in volume II of Shunya Sampadane (1) is as follows:

I do perform Linga worship so that
A Jangama should come unto my house.
If the Jangama does come unto my house
My Linga worship ceases and
The Jangama worship begins.
If you ask why:
The Linga denotes rank and reward, rebirth;
And because, in the Jangama, there is no
Rank, reward and rebirth.
Worship of Linga is no duty, but
Jangama worship is.
Between Linga and Jangama,
Jangama is pre-eminent.
Saying that, O Kudala Sangama Deva,
Henceforth I will, from birth to birth,
Perform the worship of Jangama.
And place my humble head
In worship on Jaṅgama's feet.

Then Basavanna is in an eager mood to welcome Prabhudeva, goes with Appaṇṇa, Chennabasavanna, Bācharasa, and other Sharanas, to personally welcome Prabhudeva.

Basavanna makes his obeisance at the sight of the glorious feet of Prabhudeva. He pours out his heart overflowing with love and devotion. Basavanna realizing his mistake of 'pride', apologizes to Prabhudeva, and profusely prostrates at Prabhudeva's feet. Basavanna is at Prabhudeva's feet, but the feet are intangible! Basavanna could not grasp the real form and majesty of Prabhudeva. Basavanna feels utterly helpless. This awakens him to the sense of his ignorant vices and errors. Basavanna is great because he admits his faults without reserve.

In Shunya Sampadane, all this obeisance is given in 15 consecutive vachanas of Basavanna. One of the vachanas is as follows:

In all the three-fold ways I have erred, Sir!
But once show mercy to me, Lord!
If having known this I should err,
Do with me as Thou please,
O Kudala Sangama Deva!

Then there is Basavanna's inquiry by Prabhudeva. Allama Prabhudeva at this juncture, is very critical about such faltering by Basavanna, and kind of chastises him. It seems that Allama Prabhudeva is making sure that Basavanna has well understood the concept of Pre-eminence of Jangama.

Shunya Sampadane gives Prabhudeva's fifteen vachanas of enquiry. And in this enquiry, in another 23 of his vachanas, Basavanna explains in sincere humility and submits his profound remorse. Basavanna surrenders all he had and was without reserve (1).

Basavanna is great because he admits his faults without reserve, and states that he will not make that mistake again. He also says that Kinnara Bommaṇṇa serves as his witness. This vachana 46 in this chapter of Shunya Sampadane is as follows:

My mistakes are numerous without an end:
There are no bounds to your patience!
By your feet, I swear, I will not err again!
O Kudala Sangama Deva,
Before Thy Ancients,
Let Kinnara Bommaṇṇa's feet be witness!

Allama Prabhudeva continues being critical of Basavanna. Vachana 60 in this chapter as referenced in is as follows:

Once you believe that Jangama is Linga,
You should be cleared of all doubt.
When all doubt has ceased, look,
This true devotion has turned upon its tracks!

Where one is humble for a little while

And then a little while is filled with self-pride
Look, our Guheshvara-Linga holds aloof!

This enquiry continues. Then Basavanna brings Siddharamayya into the fray in one of his vachanas. Vachana 77 in this chapter is as follows:

Look, Lord,
You only are my reason and resort!
Look, Lord,
You only are my Guru and supreme-Guru!
Look, Lord,
You only are the Light within my soul!
O Kudala Sangama Deva,
Thy Sharana Siddharamayya knows
Thou only art my Guru, Thy disciple I.
Please come Prabhu!

After that, Kinnara Bommaṇṇa, Siddharamayya, Chennabasavanna and Maḍivāḷa Māchidēva come to Basavanna's rescue. They all have their own vachanas supporting Basavanna (1).

Allama Prabhudeva, then completely satisfied, praises Basavanna. Vachana 82 on page 203 in volume II of Shunya Sampadane (1) is as follows:

I found my ancient teacher in
What is Come (Āyata).
I found my ancient teacher in
What is Made One's Own (Svāyata).
I found my ancient teacher in

What Inhabits One (Sannahita).
Hail! O hail to Thy holy feet,
My ancient teacher Sangana Basavanna
Abiding in Guheshvara-Linga!

'What is come' is Linga, 'what is made one's own' is Linga, and 'what inhabits one' is Linga.

It is notable indeed that the vachanas very well depict the concept of pre-eminence of Jangama over anything else. The vachanas establish the concept that Jangama is Linga and Linga is Jangama. One worships Linga so that a Jangama should come to one's house; when the Jangama comes, the Linga worship stops and the Jangama worship begins; this is because, between Linga and Jangama, Jangama is pre-eminent. When Jangama comes, one should receive Jangama as the Divinity Itself, not as an ordinary person.

Upon seeing sincerity and humility in Basavanna, Prabhudeva, now content, accepts the invitation and enters Basavanna's place. Prabhudeva then discusses the nature of true-bhakti with Basavanna and the Sharanas. Prabhudeva sings the praise of Basavanna's glory in various ways. Basavanna is awed into unspeakable wonder at the sublime stature of Prabhudeva. Basavanna, then in his turn, sings the glories of his Jangama-Guru Prabhudeva.

There are 93 vachanas in this fifth chapter. The subtotal so far comes to 395 vachanas.

Chapter 6

SAMPĀDANE OF MARUḶUSHAṄKARADĒVA

The sixth chapter describes the instant recognition of spiritual eminence of Maruḷushaṅkaradēva by Prabhudeva.

Maruḷushaṅkaradēva is said to have come from a place that is the present day Afghanistan or the Orissa State in India. He apparently was well versed in the Veerashaiva lore before coming to the city of Kalyana. In Kalyana, he did not want to be noticed by other Sharanas although he moved around among them, and came to know them well. Maruḷushaṅkaradēva's spiritual eminence was not noticed by other Sharanas including Basavanna for about 12 years. He was looked upon as an ordinary person. He was deeply versed in the Prasada lore, since he could experience the Divine Grace in the crumbs of the Sharanas. Prabhudeva, soon after his arrival there, and then seeing Maruḷushaṅkaradēva, instantly notices his spiritual eminence.

At that juncture, Maruḷushaṅkaradēva cheerfully steps forward and makes obeisance to Prabhudeva. Vachana 10 on pages 243 and 244 in volume II of Shunya Sampadane (1) is as follows:

Hail! Hail! O save me, save!
Lord, I waited even as the baby waits
Nine months in the womb.

O Lord, today my birth has at last borne fruit!
O shuddha, siddha, prasiddha,
Prasanna Prabhu, Shāntamallikārjuna Lord,
By Basavarāja's mercy I have seen
Prabhudeva's face and I am saved!
Thine is the grace, it is thine!
To all the ancient saints I humbly bow.

Now that Prabhudeva has come to Kalyana, Maruḷushaṅkaradēva feels that his worldly bonds have been broken, his ignorance has been swept away, and delusion of his mind has completely disappeared. He feels that the eternal Light Divine has shone upon him at last.

Prabhudeva expresses his profound admiration of the great Maruḷushaṅkaradēva. One of Prabhudeva's vachanas, vachana 14 on pages 247 and 248 in volume II of reference 1 is as follows:

Oh to have seen this hero without pluck!
Oh to have seen this lover without youth!
Oh to have seen this valor without arms!
Oh to have seen
This fragrance without flower!
In Guheshvara-Linga to have beheld
The name called Maruḷushaṅkara!

Maruḷushaṅkaradēva attains Aikya, the unitive state, and continues to praise Allama Prabhudeva.

Basavanna is bewildered. He states that he can understand the formless life-force attaining Shunya, but is perplexed at how the gross body also could attain the Absolute.

Prabhudeva then explains: **Sharaṇa has no karmic body**; Sharana, though in this world, is not of it; Sharana is not of the visible world; **Sharaṇa is above the bodily nature; Sharana is not the one who enjoys rewards set forth in the Āgamas**; and such explanations.

Basavanna and Chennabasavanna then praise the glory of Maruḷushaṅkaradēva.

There are 51 vachanas in this sixth chapter, and the subtotal comes to 446 vachanas.

Chapter 7

BASAVESHVARA'S SAMPĀDANE

In this seventh chapter Prabhudeva leads Basavanna, in his discussion, into the field of **Oneness Philosophy of the Sharanas where knowledge and devotion are perfectly harmonized.**

Prabhudeva, Siddharamayya and the Sharanas are all in Basavanna's place. Basavanna feels extremely happy to see the gathering together of the Sharanas, and is ecstatic that Prabhudeva the Great Jangama is in the assembly of the Sharanas.

Basavanna states that just being in the company of Sharanas, his body, his mind, his possessions, and his entire being are all made pure, and have become a great receptacle for the Divine. Prabhudeva fully appreciates Basavanna's reverence for the Sharanas, and he leads Basavanna in his discussion.

Prabhudeva remarks that:

- It is difficult to conquer Māyā (pronounced as Maayaa) even for gods if they are born on earth wearing a body.
- Karma pursues those who think that after dispelling the ignorance of the mind, happiness can be achieved by meditation, and forgetfulness plagues those who try to meditate.

- In the advancement of Yoga all the activities of the mind must be stilled in order to meditate or contemplate.

Basavanna is of the opinion that meditation can conquer Maya and that meditation can achieve anything.

Prabhudeva comments that:

- Māyā can never be dispelled by meditation, only Divine Grace can do that.
- Meditation by itself cannot reveal the Divine Reality.
- The Absolute is beyond the range of either the body or mind.

Then Prabhudeva asks Basavanna, in what manner he has harbored in his mind/heart the 'Thing' beyond speech and thought.

Basavanna replies this way: 'The Lord's Maya encompasses the world, but my mind encompasses the Lord; the Lord is mightier than the world, but I am mightier than the Lord; I have held the Lord in me, like the reflection of an elephant in a mirror'.

Prabhudeva then responds by saying: 'If you say He is lodged within you, then He is beyond the spirit's worshipping; if you say He dwells outside you, then He is not bound by outer acts; if you say He is lodged in consciousness, then your reason cannot cope with Him; how can you see Shunya where there is no sense of being, and what method is there which can help know Shunya and become one with It?'

Basavanna understands the force of Prabhudeva's argument and yields to him by saying that the Guru has wiped out the nature and qualities of Basavanna's body and mind; the result is that the two have become one. This undivided being according to Basavanna is Prabhudeva. Since the Lord has taken the seat in the innermost shrine of his being, all inward and outward activities are ascribed to the Lord, and there is no trace of his body and mind left.

Prabhudeva continues to pressure Basavanna. He says: Through union the body was born; that body bred ignorance; out of ignorance the sense of 'You' and 'I' arose. If the outer is you and the inner is me, without this sense of duality if you say you have known Him by yourself, contradicts your thought. Deceptive play of knowing and not-knowing has no ending. How does Linga abide in you? Here Prabhudeva hints that being and knowing are not different from one another. Being is knowing and knowing is being, one and the same.

Basavanna replies that knowledge and ignorance are 'He' alone by saying – 'You alone, and none else, are my awareness and my forgetfulness, my power and essence of the spirit of Shiva; you, and none else, dwell in the power of my right knowledge as Linga enjoying all things;

you, and nothing else, is this will of mine which has shed its illusion'.

Prabhudeva is not satisfied with that answer; he pressures him further. You are saying Shiva is both knowledge and ignorance, and Shiva and Shakti are both you; without knowing who you are, if you say all this is Brahman, will the Lord approve your karma-tainted word?

Basavanna tries to clarify what he means. He does not intend to attribute his knowledge and forgetfulness, his body and mind to Prabhudeva or the Lord, and himself remain as a separate and independent entity. He states that he has no separate and independent identity, thus implying complete submission in the Lord.

Prabhudeva is still not completely satisfied with the explanation. He says that the duality of Anga and Linga, and word and knowledge seem to still exist in Basavanna, and asks: 'the duality of Divine and devotee still appears in you; tell me how, losing name and form, these could become the One?'

Basavanna's submission to this is – He abides in the greatest of the great, the boundless and profound, and has become a light within the light of the Lord. Vachana 15 on page 325 in volume II of Shunya Sampadane (1) is as follows:

Greater even than the Great, O Lord,
Did I abide in the greatest of the great,
The boundless and profound!

What shall I say, O Lord,
How I became a light within the
Light of Kudala Sangama, till
My utterance was in silence bound?

This saying of greater than the great for the Absolute is in many Upanishads (14).

Prabhudeva seems to be satisfied with this submission, and praises Basavanna. Then they praise each other.

In one of the vachanas, Prabhudeva glorifies Basavanna, and says that Basavanna revealed the principles of Guru, Linga, Jangama and Prasada as different manifestations of one and the same Principle.

In yet another vachana, Prabhudeva praises Basavanna, and describes his achievement. Vachana 30 on pages 345 and 346 in volume II of Shunya Sampadane (1) is something like this:

By anointing the body with practice, you have risen above the body!

By letting the knowledge fill your innocent heart, you have risen above the mind!

Because of your dedication that has remained unbroken in content,

Your entire being has become united with Linga!

Our Guheshvara-Linga knows how you eliminated Bayalu's illusion

And tore-up the fabric of rebirth, O Sangana Basavanna!

In the above vachana, Bayalu means 'Infinite' or 'Void', and is same as Shunya.

The editors of volume II of Shunya Sampadane give the following explanation for this vachana:

Sad-bhakti means true bhakti, real bhakti, or pure bhakti. The Veerashaiva sad-bhakti requires not only the liberation of the soul, but also the liberation of the body, life and mind. What is more important is that these three – body, life and mind – are to be made into the nature of the Divine, and then be united with the Divine. The body is to be emptied of its earthliness, and then filled with Divine nature which is āchāra or practice; it is to be elevated to the position of the Linga; this is the liberation of the body. The mind of the Bhakta is to be delivered out of ignorance, and then be filled with Divine knowledge. One has to incorporate the Divine expression of love, knowledge, power, bliss and peace, into one's inner and outer being, and have these functioning through one's body, life and mind.

This is in contrast to Shankaracharya's Advaita Philosophy (23) which considers the body and the world as a whole to be insignificant, and the spiritual seeker is advised to focus exclusively on the inner Self.

Further, most Hindus view the body to be a breeding ground for karma and an automatic hindrance to enlightenment. According to the Hindu view of life, the individual soul takes the body as a result of *Sañchita karma* that had accumulated from actions/deeds performed in the past life, and experiences the consequences of those actions – enjoying the fruits of good deeds and suffering as a result of bad deeds.

This latter part of this chapter emphasizes the Veerashaiva Philosophy: ***The whole universe including the physical body of a person is a manifestation of the Divine, and the body is a temple that enshrines the Divine Linga. One has to recognize the immanence of Linga in one's body, and understand the importance of the body in the process of realization of the Self.***

In response to Prabhudeva praising Basavanna, the latter remarks that 'Through you I learned all the right doctrines'. Vachana 36 on pages 354 and 355 in volume II of Shunya Sampadane (1) is as follows:

Who has revealed to me, Sir, that
Linga is Jangama and Jangama is Linga?
Because by Linga-worship
There is no breaking the wheel of births,
You came in Jangama-Linga guise;
You taught me and protected me;
Showed me what in me is
Create and increate;

Convinced me that Pranalinga is Jangama.
And because you showed me this,
O Kudala Sangama Deva,
Through you I am saved;
That is so, Prabhu!

That is the last vachana in this chapter. The seventh chapter has 36 vachanas. The subtotal so far comes to 482 vachanas.

The third volume starts with the eighth chapter.

Chapter 8

CHENNABASAVESHVARA'S SAMPĀDANE

Chennabasaveshvara in the above title of the eighth chapter stands for Chennabasavanna. It is said that Chennabasavanna was a man of extraordinary gifts of intellect and holiness, and of precocious wisdom.

Chennabasavaṇṇa

The editors of volume III of the referenced Shunya Sampadane (1) give the following information about Chennabasavanna:

Chennabasavanna was Basavanna's nephew. He was the son of Basavanna's elder sister Nāgalāmbike who was also called Akkanāgamma. His father was Shivadēva who was also known as Shivasvāmi. Chennabasavanna's parents had accompanied Basavanna to Kappaḍi Kudala Sangama where they had looked after Basavanna in his younger days. Later they had accompanied Basavanna to the city of Kalyana.

Chennabasavaṇṇa grew up under the guidance of Basavaṇṇa. Basavaṇṇa was considered as his Guru. Chennabasavaṇṇa seems to have been very adept in Sanskrit and the Sanskrit scriptures. It is not clear whether someone other than Basavaṇṇa, like Chennabasavaṇṇa's father Shivadēva

(Shivasvāmi), also was involved in teaching Sanskrit scriptures to Chennabasavaṇṇa. There are many Sanskrit inserts of various Sanskrit scriptures in Chennabasavaṇṇa's vachanas.

Though Chennabasavanna was quite young in age, he was very mature in knowledge and spiritual experience. He was very prominent in the discussions at the Anubhava Mantapa where Shatsthala Philosophy was discussed. The main part of the referenced Shunya Sampadane (1), in the prose section on page 26 of volume II, states that Chennabasavanna was the cause for expounding (explaining/interpreting) the Shatsthala doctrine to all the Saints (eminent Pioneers). The editors of volume II of the same reference (1), in the explanatory notes on page 359, state that, drawing mainly on the knowledge and mystic experience of the contemporary Sharanas, Chennabasavanna systematized the Shatsthala Philosophy.

Basavanna in one of his vachanas says that Chennabasavanna established the *'five-fold discipline (Pañchāchāra)' consisting of Guru, Linga, Jangama, Padodaka and Prasada*. Yes, the term *'Pañchāchāra'* is used here for this set of five items, not for what is in the Shivagamas.

At Kalyana, Chennabasavanna was closely associated with Basavanna and Prabhudeva. It is said that if Basavanna and Prabhudeva represent Guru and Jangama principles respectively, Chennabasavanna represents the Linga principle.

Sometimes, Chennabasavanna has been referred to as 'Chikkadonnayaka' in Shunya Sampadane. This may be because he probably had some important position as a minister under Basavanna.

Since his birth, Chennabasavanna was together with Basavanna until the very end. They had to part from each other only because of the unfortunate incident at Kalyana. The event that precipitated the unfortunate incident was the violent action by Bijjala because of the so called inter-caste marriage (see 'Basavanna' article in this book). Chennabasavanna and most of the Sharanas accompanying Chennabasavanna left Kalyana and went to Ulavi (Ulave), a village in the North Kenara District in Karnataka State, about 400 miles from Kalyana. Chennabasavanna spent his last days at Ulavi. It is said that he lived only for about 24 years and died in the year 1167 sometime after the death of Basavanna. Chennabasavanna's vachana is the last vachana in Shunya Sampadane (1) where he says 'In Lord Kūḍala-Chenna-Saṅgama, the end arrived for me as a Prasada of all the Saints!' Chennabasavanna's vachana signature is Kūḍala Chenna-Saṅgama-Dēva.

Chennabasavaṇṇa's Sampādane

While Prabhudeva and Basavanna were engaged in the discourse as in the seventh chapter above, Chennabasavanna interjects and wants to know whether Bhakta Basavanna who stands for devotion, and Jangama Prabhudeva who stands for knowledge, have achieved oneness. He comments that Basavanna believes in an ultimate positive God whereas Prabhudeva believes in an ultimate nothing that is Shunya and that both being stubborn, are they really rich in Linga.

Prabhudeva explains how there is perfect harmony between the real Bhakta Basavanna and the real Jangama Prabhudeva; they have overcome the illusion of being two, and now remain as one. Chennabasavanna sees that, though they seem to be different, in reality they are essentially one. Then all three of them go on praising one another.

In one of those vachanas of praise, Allama Prabhudeva, in the context of discussing with Chennabasavanna, explains the creation aspect. Vachana 25 on pages 43 and 44 in volume III of Shunya Sampadane (1) is as follows:

O Sir, when neither the one principle was,
Nor the diverse principles,
Nor Nature and Spirit,
As sport of soul and the Supreme,
When nothing ever was
The Void (Bayalu), congealing,
Became the single drop (Bindu).
When that drop sat on the
Three-lettered pedestal,
Om was produced.

Taking hold within that Sound was
The one Sharana;
Out of that Sharana, Nature was born,
Out of that Nature, the world.
Knowing, through Basavanna's grace,
The glory of Chennabasavanna
The Guheshvara's Sharana who
Transcending the world and all its works,
Dwells in the Reality, I say: Hail! O Hail!

Void (Bayalu) stands for the Absolute Reality. Bindu translated as the drop is symbolic of Consciousness; it is the 'sport' or 'desire' to create. The three lettered pedestal refers to the three letters 'a', 'u' and 'm' which constitute Om. Sharana is derived from the Absolute. Sharana is eternal and timeless. And everything else is derived from the Sharana.

In the following vachana, Allama Prabhudeva is asking Chennabasavanna to explain greatness of Basavanna to him. Vachana 28 on pages 47 and 48 in volume III of Shunya Sampadane (1) is like this:

This Advaita baby, on touching my palm,
Transformed me to itself;
All thought of I and me went,
And I know no other thought at all.
When I have come to shelter under you,
And to know my past through you, how can
I know the glory of Sanga's Basavanna?
Let Guheshvara bear witness,
Sanga's Basavanna shines within your heart!

Make me understand Basavanna's glory,
O Chennabasavanna.

In the above vachana, Allama Prabhudeva is saying that, **one starts with the worship of Linga on the palm, and ultimately attains oneness with the Linga itself. Once one attains this oneness, one does not have any thoughts.** Then Prabhudeva asks Chennabasavanna to explain the glory of Basavanna to him.

Another vachana says that **when one's body, knowledge, and will, are purified and offered to the divine, one realizes that the three are forms of one Divine Grace.**

When Prabhudeva remarks that Basavanna himself is the primal Sharana, Chennabasavanna exclaims that 'it is false, all false; one should not say that Basavanna is the primal Sharana; Linga is begun but Basavanna is un-begun; Linga was born of Basavanna's loins; Jangama was born of Basavanna's loins; and only when Basavanna took it, was Prasada born'.

Prabhudeva in praising Chennabasavanna says that Linga has appeared in Chennabasavanna's body not wearing illusive garb. Then Chennabasavanna responds by saying that being in the body made him to see Prabhudeva; through the body's grace Linga is found; through the body's grace Jangama is found; and through body alone the riches of Prasada are found.

Vachana 35 on page 59 in volume III of Shunya Sampadane (1) is as follows:

Through the body's grace Linga is found;
Through the body's grace Jangama is found;
Through the body alone
Are found the riches of Prasada.
O Kūḍala-Chenna-Saṅgayya,
It is because of the body that I found you!

In the above vachana **Chennabasavanna is emphasizing the importance of the body in spiritual advancement.**

When Prabhudeva comments that the realized one, having transcended the very concept of body and bodiless-ness, is completely identified with discipline, and that Chennabasavanna lives with the true discipline in every cell of his body, Chennabasavanna responds by saying that *'Basavanna has what is called Discipline, not I'.*

Prabhudeva then states that Basavanna is one who has become all forms of Linga and that Jangama-Linga, the sublimation of all human attributes including the vital breath, is Basavanna's very own breath.

Then he expresses to know more about Basavanna's discipline. Accordingly Chennabasavanna says that Guru, Linga, Jangama and Prasāda have not only been incorporated by Basavanna but also flow through him in the form of practice, and that all these have become the Divine action.

Prabhudeva then comments that as long as there is a sense of relation between Bhakta and Linga, and Bhakta and Jangama, there is a sense of you and I; that is duality and therefore a lack of one's spiritual approach.

Chennabasavanna says that Basavanna has reached the level of Realization and therefore, he is Sharana. Then in eight vachanas Chennabasavanna goes over what that means:

- A Sharana is not only unattached but also transcends the very concept of attachment and detachment.
- Sharana is unique and does not have common attributes.
- There is no sense of I in the Great-One who is in Linga; the effulgence of Linga shows in Sharana.
- A Sharana, though in the body, remains unaffected by its nature.
- Sharana is in harmony with the essential Self.
- Basavanna is the inseparable drop Bindu in the Linga; the drop is Consciousness-Light.

Prabhudeva being pleased with Chennabasavanna's presentation, praises him, and then they again praise each other.

Prabhudeva asserts that true Knowledge is not that which is acquired by common spiritual aids of Guru, Linga and such, but it is attained through oneself. **The realization of oneself is possible only when one has transcended the idea of Godhead.**

At this juncture, Chennabasavanna accuses Prabhudeva by saying 'Because you took Linga by killing Animisha, you are a traitor of the Guru'.

Prabhudeva responds 'Once the Guru's breath dissolved in Linga, that Linga came to my palm, and is in my knowledge; no treason lies against me towards my Guru'.

Chennabasavanna then says 'You say one is upon the palm and the other in the mind; therefore, for you the two still exist apart from the Linga'.

Prabhudeva responds:

'The moment the Linga on the palm entered the mind, the moment the Linga in the mind entered the highest point, the moment the highest point entered all my being, everything fused in me and there is no sense of difference.

'Once the Linga fused in me there is no two.

'When life-energy Prāṇa is kindled by the light of Liṅga thus transforming it into Prāṇaliṅga, the Aṅga is illumined by the

same Light, and all its being is aglow with Divine effulgence; there can be no duality'.

Then Prabhudeva instructs Chennabasavanna in the Prāṇaliṅga lore as follows:

- Splendor of the sacred words of the Guru is transmitted like the perfume wafted by the wind.
- The experience of the absence of all thought and form as one realizes the Ultimate, is Shunya.
- The Absolute by its own nature turns into Light.
- The splendor shining like a flawless gem is filled with Pranalinga in the nine energy-channels.
- The sound that emanates is the way to the Absolute beyond all microcosms and macrocosms above the heavens.
- To know the nature of the Supreme Self, one has to have the aid of the individual self; that is the way to the Absolute.
- To reach the Absolute Reality, one has to pass beyond both ignorance and knowledge.
- All words entailing knowledge have to completely disappear; the ultimate realization is Silence.
- When Truth and Goodness are at rest, there is no measuring of the magnitude of Pranalinga.
- The master of the six philosophical school systems (Darshanas are the six Schools of Philosophy, namely, Sāṁkhya, Nyāya, Vaishēshika, Yoga, Pūrva Mīmāmsa, and Uttara Mīmāmsa; *the*

master of these six systems means the Absolute) dwells in the innermost heart; for whomsoever it is, both earth and Heaven are the same.

- The Light of the lotus of the heart having filled with Parabrahman, points to the Supreme height of Bliss.
- For the Absolute, there is no illusion of earth, water, fire, wind and sky, which are symbolic of body, mind, vital breath, will and soul. Pranalinga experience involves complete suspension of all these.

This eighth chapter has 84 vachanas. The subtotal so far comes to 566 vachanas.

Chapter 9

MAḌIVĀḶAYYA'S SAMPĀDANE

Maḍivāḷa Māchayya, as he was known, washed Sharanas' clothes. That was his 'Kāyaka', the 'dedicated labor'. He became a close associate of Basavanna at the city of Kalyana.

Maḍivāḷa Māchayya

The editors of the referenced Shunya Sampadane (1) give the following information about Maḍivāḷa Māchayya.

Maḍivāḷa Māchayya was born at a place presently known as Dēvara Hipparagi in the Bijapur district of Karnataka. He was born in a washer-man family. It seems that he was born before 1131 CE (AD), and therefore he was an older contemporary of Basavanna. It is said that although he was a washer-man (clothes cleaner) by profession, he had a Veerashaiva initiation, and had been well educated in spirituality, philosophy and religion.

Hearing Basavanna's virtues and achievements, Māchayya came to the city of Kalyana. Once there he became a close associate of Basavanna.

He washed Sharanas' clothes. It was not just his profession, it was his dedicated labor Kāyaka. Every morning he would collect the clothes and carry them to a pond, and after washing them, bring them back to their owners. It is said that he had tied jingle bells to one of his feet so that when he was returning with washed clothes, the bell-rings would warn others so that no one else should touch the clothes he had washed.

Maḍivāḷa Māchayya played an important role in the discussions at the Academy of the Sharanas (Anubhava Mantapa) and in the whole Sharana movement. Shunya Sampadane addresses him as Father Maḍivāḷa.

Maḍivāḷa Māchayya never left Kalyana until the last fateful days. When Sharanas were forced to leave Kalyana in the year 1167 or so (see the article on Basavanna for the reason), he accompanied Chennabasavanna and other Sharanas who were going to Ulavi. But he did not go all the way to Ulavi, he diverted his journey to his birthplace, and there, after some time, breathed his last breath.

It is said that Maḍivāḷayya has 353 vachanas to his credit (3). His vachana signature is 'Kalidēvara Deva'.

Maḍivāḷayya's Sampadane

The opening verse in this ninth chapter states that Prabhudeva enlightens Maḍivāḷayya on how Guru, Linga, and Jangama are joined to one, on the nature of the right Knowledge, and on the union in the Absolute.

Allama Prabhudeva, puts Maḍivāḷa Māchayya to the test, and in his vachana asks him the following – vachana 5 on pages 133 and 134 in volume III of Shunya Sampadane (1) is as follows:

How is it Sir?
Eye in the forehead, trouble in the heart,
And all you speak is devotion's quintessence?
Do tell how is this knowledge?
How selflessness?
Forgetfulness of knowledge and sign
Is only in words.
How can Reality be possible for you?
If you can destroy the sign and yet know it,
Look, Maḍivāḷa Māchayya,
There is no Prasada unless both are lost
In Guheshvara-Linga!

In response, Maḍivāḷa Māchayya submits an account of his antecedents in his vachana – vachana 6 on pages 134 and 135 in volume III of Shunya Sampadane (1). It is as follows:

Shall I tell my origin? You know it,
I was born to the Absolute Sublime.
Shall I reveal my state of the Unbegun?
You know I was a disembodied one.
Look, since I have come down
Into this mortal world,
Because of Basavanna
I am free from body's bonds!
My body is Basavanna, my breath is

Chennabasavanna, and
My highest knowledge is you!
Behold, O Kalidēvara Deva,
Your Sharana Basavanna knows
How the word is hushed
Where twain (two) has ceased to be!

The test/discussion continues. The following information is brought out in the vachanas:

The mind is invariably affected by the lust of the body; such an infected mind cannot have love for the Divine. One must transform lust, anger, greed, infatuation, excessive pride, and jealousy into active virtues. This refinement of the body halts the fickleness of the mind. Body is to be unburdened of all its corporeal qualities; mind should stand above all passions and agitations; will should not desire for worldly rewards; and thought has to cease its wanderings on the plane of ordinary consciousness. The duality between the devotee and the Divine, or Aṅga and Liṅga, must cease.

In the process of offering, there is a sense of 'I' first. But when the sense of 'I', along with the body, mind and soul, is offered to the Divine, it becomes the true offering. When one transcends the limits of sense of both ego and ego-less-ness, that person becomes an eternal Prasadi. One experiences the body shedding the lower nature, and getting filled with the Divine becoming the vital breath. **If one is temperamental and has distress in the mind, one will not be free from pride and egoism, and will not be able to attain the Real. There is no Prasāda unless both temper and distress of the mind are rid of.**

By offering body, mind and life to Guru, Linga, and Jangama, one becomes pure, perfect, and most perfect Prasada. Such offering has to be with integral knowledge and intense devotion. One's body, mind and life are transmuted to Prasada itself.

Will and will-less-ness effect the union of the Begun and the Unbegun. **Until the will has ceased, the knowledge is not firm. Māyā is responsible for divisive ignorance and duality. Words reflecting duality are a clear sign of ignorance. Real Knowledge is possible only when all dualities have completely disappeared. Knowledge to be real and pure must transcend all these limitation. Only the enlightened consciousness can seize the Divine.**

Maḍivāḷayya, the washer-man, was able to wash off the dirt that clung to his body, mind and soul, and make everything fit for the Divine.

There are 53 vachanas in this ninth chapter. The subtotal so far comes to 619 vachanas.

Chapter 10

SIDDHARĀMAYYA'S BESTOWAL OF GRACE BY THE GURU

The great Shivayogi Siddharāma is not wearing an Ishtalinga on his body because he has not been invested with one before. As can be remembered from the third chapter above, Prabhudeva had brought Siddharamayya to the city of Kalyana promising him that he will have the truth of the Linga on the palm explained to him through Basavanna.

On the occasion when innumerable great ancients including Prabhudeva, Basavanna and Chennabasavanna held discourses, Siddharamayya requests Prabhudeva to have the truth of the Linga on the palm explained to him through Basavanna, as had Prabhudeva promised him and had brought him to the city of Kalyana for that purpose.

Prabhudeva requests Basavanna to do so, but Basavanna simply says that his heart was not pleased that there was no Anga-Linga relation in Siddharamayya. Basavanna does not explain the truth of the Ishtalinga any further.

Siddharamayya remarks that having seen in his heart the Parabrahman named Maḍivāḷayya, he has been in ecstasy. After this remark an intense discussion about Ishtalinga starts. All this discussion is in the vachanas in Shunya Sampadane.

Chennabasavanna says that unless the Linga is on the body, the peace of the Linga is not attained in the Prana; those having triple body must possess triple Linga; just as one cannot live without any one of these bodies, a true Sharana cannot do without any one of the three divisions of Linga.

The three bodies (the three anga divisions) are – the gross body, the subtle body, and the causal body. The three Liṅga divisions are - Ishtalinga, Pranalinga, and Bhāvaliṅga. The three types of anga and the three types of Linga constitute the anga-Linga relationship.

Siddharamayya responds by saying that his body, mind and knowledge have been made as one, and that in the experience of the Divine there is no 'within' and 'without'; he is free from the earthly nature.

Prabhudeva intervenes in support of Siddharamayya and says:

'What need is there for Ishtalinga, a mere symbol, for Siddharamayya through whom the very Linga breathes? What need is there for external worship for a consciousness illumined by the Light Divine? Why set boundaries of duplicity or triplicity for one who has transcended all bounds?'

Chennabasavanna responds: One cannot attain detachment unless the Linga is attached to the anga.

Prabhudeva reiterates: *When both body and soul are Divine, the outer symbol is superfluous.*

Chennabasavanna now says - Ishtalinga is the product of the process that divinizes the body, and it is a symbol embodying Pranalinga. Sharanas who know that form itself is formless, do not approve of such lack of anga-Linga relationship.

It is said that 770 immortal saints listened and favored Chennabasavanna's stand. It is also said that some of their leaders spoke to Prabhudeva scorning, challenging and denying the type of eight-fold Yoga of Siddharamayya, and saying that:

'To realize the Shiva Principle through spiritual knowledge gained by studying, examining and assimilating the Vedanta, Siddhanta, Dvaita and Shaivism was false'.

From the above statement, it can be discerned that Siddharāmayya's religious practice was based on the study of Vedanta which is mainly the Upanishads, but also Bhagavad-Gita and Brahma-sutras, Siddhanta which means doctrine, and probably refers to Siddhanta Shikhamani, Dvaita which means duality, and Shaivism philosophy which probably refers to the

Shivagama texts. All these scriptures are in the Sanskrit language. Apparently this was not acceptable to the notable Sharana leaders.

Prabhudeva then tells Siddharamayya that those innumerable saints, Chennabasavanna chief among them, would not approve admittance to the Sharana community unless one had the Linga on the person. And therefore Prabhudeva advises him to have invested with the Ishtalinga.

Siddharamayya overwhelmed by various arguments of the Sharanas, and with the advice of Prabhudeva, agrees to undergo the procedure of initiation, and requests Prabhudeva to make the grace available to him through Basavanna and Chennabasavanna. Prabhudeva then asks Chennabasavanna to do the honor.

Accordingly Chennabasavanna bestows initiation upon Siddharamayya. It is described in one of his vachanas – vachana 49 on pages 258 and 259 in volume III of Shunya Sampadane (1):

- First, the three taints or impurities are wiped out by the Grace of the Guru. The impurities are - *āṇavamala* which is known as primordial dirt that subsists in the soul, and keeps the soul separate from the Divine; *māyāmala* which is associated with Maya that masks/hides the real nature of the inner self; and *kārmikamala* which is associated with the soul, and which makes one to enjoy or suffer according to the good or bad deeds.

- After that, the Guru performs 21 kinds of initiations; they are grouped into 3 main categories with 7 kinds of initiations in each:
- The corporeal initiation is related to the body. The 7 corporeal initiations are – that of command where it is deemed of the disciple not to go the way of the world; that which employs analogies where the Guru reveals to the disciple the eight-fold counterparts to the external protective shields in the inner being of the person, namely, awareness, right knowledge, self-experience, nectar of compassion, gift of Prasada, self-conscious splendor, self-conscious light, and self-conscious bliss; that which bids sit upon a throne; that which is done sprinkling holy water from the pot; that which consists of ashen crown; Linga coming to the palm; and incorporation of the Linga itself.
- The second group of 7 vital initiations consist of – conformity to the code; un-worldliness; effacement of oneself; the teachings of the principles; teaching of spiritual lore; the grace; and purity in the Truth.
- The third group of 7 mental (mind) initiations consists of – one-pointed mind; firm vows; dedication of the five-fold senses; non-violence; absorption of the mind; oneness with Linga; and liberation here and now.
- This is said to be the natural initiation relating the possession of triple Linga to the trinity of body, life, and mind.

Siddharamayya thereupon rejoices:

...When Guru reduced the infinite Shiva-Linga to a point and set it on the palm, what other Yoga is there?

...When you performed the Linga worship and took the grace from Jangama, would your new illumined mind accept mere Yoga?

...And I, by his grace, have shed the customary forms of Yoga, and found in Shiva-Yoga-Eternity, the Shatsthala consisting of Bhakta, Maheshvara, Prasadi, Pranalingi, Sharana and Aikya, and have become qualified for the fellowship *(Adhikāri).*

Siddharamayya achieves the contact between his anga and Linga.

After the above, there are many vachanas of praise. The Sharanas praise one another.

This tenth chapter has 108 vachanas; the subtotal comes to 727 vachanas.

Chapter 11

PRABHUDĒVA'S APOTHEOSIS

In this eleventh chapter, Prabhudeva is worshipped and adored by Basavanna and the other Sharanas. When Prabhudeva gladly comes to the inner chamber of Basavanna's house, the Sharanas sing praise of the great Prabhudeva the 'Supreme Guru'.

It is said that, although traditional ritual instruments are mentioned in this worship, the instruments are to be taken not as material items but as spiritual offerings. For example, water is to be considered as Supreme Bliss not as water, and incense to be considered as Right Knowledge not as incense itself.

It is said that, when Prabhudeva graced Basavanna's place with his presence, Basavanna did the following: hung festoons of pearls; spread a carpet of clean silk; tied up a canopy glittering with the nine gems set in it; painted the patterns on the floor after six-fold cleaning of the floor; welcomed Prabhudeva with five large musical instruments; sang in auspicious tunes with superabundant joy holding aloft the waving light of pearls and rubies; held out his hand while Maḍivāḷayya said aloud "He comes! Attention to his feet!", and bowed down to Prabhudeva as he entered and took his seat.

Then Basavanna's worship is described in his vachana – vachana 2 on pages 331 through 333 in volume III of Shunya Sampadane (1):

"When the Supreme Guru sat upon the throne made of alchemic stone, I adored his feet with water of the Supreme Bliss; I smeared him with Divine perfume; I laid upon him rice grains of the Imperishable; I worshipped him with the flower of the heart's lotus, fanning him with incense made of scent of the Right Knowledge; offered him by way of ritual gifts, the essence of devotion; poured to wash his hands, the Highest Joy; gave him, for his tambūlam, the triple purity; and so, through consubstantial union, the grace of Prabhudeva came down to me!"

Then Basavanna sings as he waves the propitiatory lamp on the occasion. The song starts with *'Jaya! Jaya! Shri Mahādēva!'* sung three times; it means *'Hail! Hail! To the glorious Great God!'* Then the song continues with many mystic words taken from the Vedas – *'Om bhūḥ Om bhuvaḥ...bhargō dēvasya dhīmahi'*.

The mystic words *'bhūḥ, bhuvah, and suvah'* are explained as follows: Taittirīya Upanishad (21) I.5.1 says - Bhūh, Bhuvah and Suvah are the three celebrated mystical utterances. What is called *Bhūh* stands for this world, the fire, the sacred verses called Riks (of Rigveda), and the air that is breathed in (*Prāṇaḥ*). What is denoted as *Bhuvah* stands for the intermediate space between heaven and earth, the air, the Sāman chants (of Sāmaveda), and the air that is breathed out (*Apānaḥ*). What is noted as *Suvah* stands for heaven, the sun, the sacrificial formulae called Yajus (of Yajurveda), and the vital airs that sustains life when the breath is arrested (*Vyānaḥ*). These mystic words are also in many other Upanishads such as Chandogya Upanishad (13) II.23.2 and Brihadaranyaka Upanishad (8) VI.4.25.

The mystic words *'bhargō dēvasya dhīmahi'* are part of the famous Gayatri Mantra which is the celebrated verse of the three Vedas - Rigveda III.62.10; Shukla Yajurveda (it comes four times in this Veda) III.35; XXII.9; XXX.2; and XXXVI.3; and Samaveda 1462. These words have been translated as *'may we attain the glory of the Divine'.*

The full Gayatri Mantra has been translated to mean something like this (11, 12, 24, 25, 26 and 27):

'Let us contemplate the beautiful splendor of Savitur the Devine, who may inspire our visions'

After Basavanna does homage to Prabhudeva with eight forms of worship and sixteen kinds of service, Chennabasavanna, having done obeisance and worship, receives the symbolic Padodaka which is the Supreme Bliss.

Shunya Sampadane does not explain *'Padodaka'* anywhere, but it does use the term Padodaka for its symbolic meaning *'Supreme-*

Bliss'. This comes about mainly in this eleventh chapter. It is as follows:

First Basavanna adores Prabhudeva in his vachana (vachana 2 described above) and says something like this:

'...I adored his feet with water of the Supreme Bliss...'

Then Chennabasavanna performs obeisance to Prabhudeva and says something like this in his vachana – vachana 8 on page 335 in volume III of Shunya Sampadane (1):

'When a Jangama called Supreme Consciousness comes to the house of a Bhakta known as the Eternal One,

The Bhakta performs the feet worship with waterless-water.

That Padodaka is the Great Padodaka.

The Pure-Bliss converting to water and washing his lotus feet can liberate one who drinks that water.

This being so, having received that Padodaka, I found Peace'.

The Veerashaivas do not perform ritualistic ceremonies with literal Padodaka. They use the term Padodaka for its symbolic meaning which is 'Supreme-Bliss'.

After Chennabasavanna paid homage to Prabhudeva and worshipped him, Chennabasavanna experienced the highest joy.

Following Chennabasavanna's obeisance, other Sharanas, one by one, paid their homage to Prabhudeva, and obtained grace from him. It is said that it was not just homage and worship by them, there was dancing and singing.

After all that obeisance and worship the Sharanas praised Prabhudeva, and then they praised one another.

There are 57 vachanas in this eleventh chapter. The subtotal so far comes to 784 vachanas.

Chapter 12

ĀYDAKKI MĀRAYYA'S SAMPĀDANE

In the opening verse at the beginning of this twelfth chapter, the composer Gūḷūra Siddhavīraṇārya says that he tells the story of Mārayya who gathered rice-grain, only a handful at a time, and then was offering it to the Sharanas with all devotion.

The popular saying *'kāyakave Kailāsa'* which means 'dedicated labor is Kailāsa', comes in Āydakki Mārayya's vachana.

The term ***'kāyaka'*** ordinarily means something related to the body. In the Sharana system of life, it means dedicated manual labor. The labor may extend to the mental or intellectual field. More importantly, the fruits of one's labor are to be offered to God/God-kind first, and not looked upon as a means for maintaining oneself or one's family. A Sharana works and lives for God. Sharana is always moving towards the Divine Life. Becomes more and more awake to all-enveloping and all-pervading Reality. And comes to realize that one lives for God, moves for God, and has one's being in God.

'Kailāsa' is the abode of Shiva. Kailāsa is a mountain in the Himalayas. In the present day, the Kailāsa Mountain is in the Autonomous Tibetan

Region of China. 'Kailāsa' is also spelled as 'Kailash'.

Shiva of the Sharanas is not a separate entity living on a mountain called Kailāsa in the Himalayas. The Sharanas consider that the body of a Sharana is the Kailāsa, the abode of Shiva. The very popular saying *'kāyave Kailāsa'* comes in many vachanas. ***'Kaya'*** means physical body of a person. **Body of a Sharana is Kailāsa, and Shiva is enshrined in the body as Linga. There is no separate Kailāsa or heaven.** This has been well explained in the Vachanas.

It is to be pointed out to the readers that the saying *'kāyakave Kailāsa'* does not come in Basavanna's vachanas. But, Basavanna has a vachana which says *'good-work is heaven'* using the Kannada words *'āchārave svarga'*. Svarga means heaven; it does not mean Shiva's abode. The other popular saying *'kāyave Kailāsa'* comes in the vachanas of Basavanna and Allama Prabhudeva.

Mārayya and his wife Lakkamma

The following information is in the introductory article provided by the editors of the volume IV of the referenced Shunya Sampadane.

Mārayya, later known as Āydakki Mārayya, was one of the great Sharanas of the 12th century. Although his Sharana life story has been depicted in many Sharana biographies and Veerashaiva

Puranas, not much is known about his childhood and upbringing.

It is believed that Mārayya is from a village in the Raichur District in Karnataka where there is a shrine of Amarēshvara. Thus he uses the term 'Amarēshvara-Linga' for the Absolute Divinity he refers to, and uses it as his vachana signature.

It seems that Mārayya was drawn to the city of Kalyana by the great movement launched by Basavanna. He settles there in Kalyana with his wife Lakkamma. It is said that, by then, Mārayya probably was not much less than fifty years of age.

Every day Mārayya would pick up spilled rice and other grains, from the streets of Kalyana and the courtyard of Basavanna's place. For this he was known as Āydakki Mārayya. Lakkamma would cook using the collected grains and serve the food to Sharanas. Afterwards, Mārayya would go to the Anubhava Mantapa, the Academy of Sharanas, and listen to the discourses with deep interest. Lakkamma also would do the same; her motto was duty first and discourses afterwards. For some years, their presence was not noticed.

The main part of Shunya Sampadane picks up the story from here.

Sampadane of Mārayya and Lakkamma

Mārayya's daily routine was to pick up spilled rice and other grains from the streets of

Kalyana and the courtyard of Basavanna's place. Mārayya's wife Lakkamma would then cook using the collected grains and serve the food to Sharanas.

One morning, before picking up the grains for the daily meal, Mārayya goes to the Sharana assembly in the Anubhava Mantapa to ascertain whether his way of doing dedicated work (kāyaka) and service (dāsōha) would take him to the Divine. This time he actively participates in the discussion with Allama Prabhudeva.

Āydakki Mārayya elaborates his view of the nature of dedicated labor to Prabhudeva. He describes his concept of Kāyaka in several vachanas. Some examples are given here.

Āydakki Mārayya's vachana which has the saying *'Kāyakave Kailāsa'*, - vachana 1 on pages 14 and 15 in volume IV of Shunya Sampadane (1) is as follows:

One who is engaged in dedicated work
Must forget the Guru's sight,
Must forget the Linga-worship,
And even if the Jangama stands in front
The obligation must be snapped.
Because such ***kāyaka is Kailāsa****.*
Amarēshvara-Linga must also do it.

In this vachana, Mārayya states that while engaged in kāyaka, one should not mind anybody, even if it is Guru, Linga or Jangama. They are all working with the One, as they are not exempt from kāyaka. This is because he says *'kāyakave Kailāsa'.*

In this saying, the Kannada word 'Kailāsa' is interpreted as Heaven. The saying, *'dedicated work is heaven',* is to be interpreted as – 'while doing dedicated work, one creates heaven right here on earth'. It is not to be interpreted as – one goes to heaven after death by doing dedicated work (28). It has been pointed out above that Kailāsa actually is a mountain in the Himalayas, and it is the abode of Shiva. Shaivas consider the abode of Shiva as heaven.

In another vachana, Āydakki Mārayya makes the point that the labor should never fetch more than what it is worth; may get less, but never more. Vachana 2 on page 15 in volume IV of Shunya Sampadane (1) is something like this:

Doing a penny's worth of work
If you ask for a bag of money
Is that the idea of true work?
To ask less than what your work is worth
That is the work done with a pure mind
For Amarēshvara-Linga.

Things earned by dedicated labor are holy. Things earned with avarice are unholy.

The concept of the dedicated labor (kāyaka) can be summarized as follows:

- First, in the name of service to God, one should never beg. Such a beggar moves away from, rather than towards, realization.
- Second, while engaged in kāyaka, one should not mind anybody, even if it is Guru, Linga or Jangama; they are all working with the One, as they are not exempt from kāyaka.
- Third, the labor of a Sharana should never fetch more than it is worth; may get less, but never more.
- Furthermore, it is incumbent upon the Sharana to do kāyaka with a pure heart and mind, and always put Sharana's best into the work. This is how one tries to express the Divine in oneself through one's work.
- Such work should never be motivated by greed or egoistic self. It is always dedicated to the Divine.
- Dāsōha, the dedicated service is closely associated with kāyaka. The work and all the earnings from work must first be offered to God. Since God is formless, the offerings are directed through the godly – Guru, Jangama and the community of Sharanas. The Sharanas' activities are driven by this profound sense of service – Dāsōha.

After Mārayya elaborates his view of the nature of dedicated labor as above, Prabhudeva indicates to Mārayya that there is more to it than just kāyaka and dāsōha.

Prabhudeva's vachana – vachana 9 on page 20 in volume IV of Shunya Sampadane (1) – is as follows:

The deed you do must lead to
The knowledge of the other Thing.
Both faith and knowledge
Must be joined in one.
When the faith has joined with knowledge
You must, after razing the stark error out,
Attain the ultimate Reality in our
Guheshvara-Linga!

A Sharana completely absorbed in the work and service will not be aware of the Reality nearest to the one. One must reach beyond 'I am the doer' and 'I am the server'. One must reach the profound depths where there is no sense of the 'I', and must try to reach the depths of silence where the mind's strivings have ceased. Mārayya accepts Prabhudeva's explanation, and fully appreciates its deep significance.

By then, Mārayya's wife Lakkamma comes looking for him, and reminds him that the daily task should not be neglected. Accordingly, Mārayya bows to the Sharanas and rushes away to collect the grains. In this hurry, he gathers a lot more grain than the usual daily quantity, and brings it home. Lakkamma was astonished to find that he had brought so much more rice. She remarks that it was greed, and that it implies poverty. True lover of God is not poor. To love is to be rich. With this she commands him to drop back the surplus rice where he had picked it up from. He complies.

The couple continue their quest to feed the Sharanas including Basavanna, Prabhudeva and other notables. Lakkamma somehow comes to know what each Sharana likes, and prepares the dishes to suit each one of them. The Sharanas were wonder-struck at the couple's devotion to kāyaka and dāsōha. Even Basavanna expresses that, although they were poor in wealth, they were richly endowed with a great heart.

Mārayya was wholly dedicated to the Divine, leading his life in conformity with the Shatsthala system. Fortunately for him, he had found in his wife Lakkamma, an ardent and pious soul. She even surpassed her husband in her progress towards self-realization.

Mārayya wanted to know from Lakkamma, how he could merge with the Linga. She responds by saying that, if work and dedication take one to Heaven/Kailāsa, the Heaven is just a worker's wage; it does not lead that person to become one with the Divine. Vachana 25 on page 32 in volume IV of Shunya Sampadane (1) is something like this:

If you think work and generosity take you to Heaven,

Is Heaven a worker's wage?

If, with no thought of what is coming or gone,

You stay engrossed in what you do,
Then Heaven is where
Mārayyapriya Amarēshvara-Linga is.

If work and dedication take one to heaven, then the heaven is just a worker's wage; it does not lead to the union with the Divine. This is an important concept of the Sharanas. It is not that Sharana wants to go to Heaven after death; Sharana's goal is to be one with the Absolute in this very life while still alive and to become the Absolute itself.

Lakkamma continues her advice: All desire in any form or guise is to be eliminated. Once the sense of 'I' and 'do' are gone, the service to Guru, Linga and Jangama itself will lead one to the Absolute. One should tread the path with one's own legs. Devotion illuminated by knowledge, unless translated into action, is no devotion. Knowledge, devotion and action should go hand in hand.

Lakkamma, in the following vachana brings up the point that **the bodies of husband and wife may be different, but they are not separate for knowledge. They are one in soul.** Vachana 32 on pages 37 and 38 in volume IV of Shunya Sampadane (1) is as follows:

Whichever way the seed may drop,
Does the sprout face this way or that?
When you forget, and I am aware,
Does that make us to be separate?

When the root perishes,
The sprout ceases to grow.

The wife and husband
Are but different in name for union;
But does that make a difference
For knowledge too?
Do not go astray,
If you would know
Mārayyapriya Amarēshvara-Linga!

Mārayya was then fully ripe for the Divine union. The couple was great in their own way – **they had two bodies with one great soul**. As true-bhakti became manifest in Mārayya, he became one with the Supreme Divine. Lakkamma with her profound knowledge and her unshakable faith in things divine soon followed in the undivided perfect Absolute.

In this context of husband and wife being in unison, Prabhudeva remarks to Basavanna, that he is convinced that the hearts of the couple are fused into one, and the sense of dual-being is gone.

Prabhudeva's vachana – vachana 45 on page 49 in volume IV of Shunya Sampadane (1) – is as follows:

As in sun-vision the twin-eyed look,
When a married couple stands
With their hearts made one,
There is dedication to Guheshvara-Linga
O Sangana Basavanna!

The couple was great in their own way – they had two bodies but they had only one great soul.

For explaining the above vachana of Prabhudeva, the editors of volume IV of Shunya Sampadane, give reference to the Rigveda verse X.191.4. It is the very last verse of the 10,589 verses of Rigveda (11, 12). It is as follows:

Common be your intentions,
Common be your hearts,
And common be your thoughts,
So that there may be
Thorough union among you.

This Rigveda verse is usually recited at the beginning of an assembly or a meeting, or even at a gathering of worshippers. It may also be recited at a wedding.

There are 54 vachanas in this twelfth chapter. The subtotal so far comes to 838 vachanas.

Chapter 13

MŌḶIGAYYA'S SAMPĀDANE

Basavanna's great religious movement at the city of Kalyana attracted seekers and scholars from all parts of India. So great was the attraction that Kashmir king Mahādevarāya and his wife Mahadevi renounced their kingdom and all their wealth to the life of Sharanas at Kalyana. They were convinced that that was the only way to the Absolute; and that the search for the Divine, its realization and practice, outweighed all the hardship.

Kashmir King and his Wife

The editors of the volume IV of Shunya Sampadane (1) give the following information about the Kashmir King Mahādevarāya and his wife Mahadevi.

Kashmir is in the north-north-western part of India. Father of Mahādevarāya, king Bhāḷalochana, ruled the Kashmir kingdom from the capitol city of Māṇḍavyapura. King Bhāḷalochana has been credited for providing to his son Mahādevarāya an excellent education that embodied many virtues – modesty, generosity and valor.

Prince Mahādevarāya became extremely pious. When coming of age, married Mahadevi, and after his father's death assumed the rule of the kingdom. He ruled for many years. He continued his worship of Linga, and it is said that he fed six to twelve thousand Jangamas every day.

The religious movement at the city of Kalyana in Karnataka which is in the southern part of India, and Basavanna's greatness attracted these Jangamas from Kashmir. When Basavanna 'brought them away' to Kalyana, the king Mahādevarāya at first became infuriated and unsuccessfully tried to get them back.

Basavanna's great religious movement at Kalyana attracted seekers and scholars from all parts of India.

Brother of the king's Guru, likewise, had gone to Kalyana. When the Guru's brother returned from Kalyana, the king offered him presents as a token of his devotion. But the gifts were not accepted – only the things earned by one's own dedicated labor (kāyaka) would be acceptable. To overcome this issue, the king disguising himself, worked at a blacksmith's workshop, and from what he had earned, obtained an item made out of iron, and offered it to the brother of his Guru. It was accepted.

All this made the king realize that the Sharana way of life is the only way to the Absolute. The king decided to go to Kalyana for good. In order to go to Kalyana and live there as a

Sharana for the rest of his life, he renounced all his wealth and his kingdom in favor of his son Liṅgarati.

As the king Mahādevarāya prepared to depart for Kalyana, he requested his wife to stay behind in Kashmir. But his wife refused, indicating that her place is at the husband's side. She accompanied him to Kalyana.

This older couple braved all the hardships of the long journey of more than 1,500 miles. Those days in the twelfth century, this type of journey was extremely difficult. The journey took many months to complete.

Kashmir King and his Wife at Kalyana

Basavanna's great religious movement at Kalyana attracted seekers and scholars from all parts of India. So great was the attraction that Kashmir king Mahādevarāya and his wife Mahadevi renounced all their wealth and their kingdom to the life of Sharanas at Kalyana. They were convinced that that was the only way to the Absolute; and that the search for the Divine, its realization and practice, outweighed all the hardship.

At Kalyana, the king changed his name to Mārayya, and his wife was known as Mahādēviyamma. He had not brought any of his belongings. He started his work as a firewood gatherer. Every morning he would go to the forest, gather the wood sticks, tie them up into a bundle, carry the bundle on his head, and sell it for a price in strict accordance with the spirit of true and honest labor. For this he came to be known as Mōḷige Mārayya, or Mōḷigeya Mārayya, or simply, Mōḷigayya.

He spent his earnings for the service of the Sharanas. Occasionally he would go to the Anubhava Mantapa and participate in the discussions. He became a prominent figure in this Sharana Assembly.

His wife Mahādēviyamma was to him the perfect helpmate and companion. They would hold discussions pertaining to the Life Divine at home in the evenings. The Jangamas after feasting at Basavanna's place would sometimes visit their house where Mahādēviyamma would serve them porridge made of rice or jawar. This simple dish apparently tasted better than what they had at Basavanna's place.

Basavanna was deeply moved when he came to know the couple's service – a true dāsōhi (one whose life is dedicated to service) in this former king who is now a simple laborer.

Sampadane of Mōḷigayya and his wife Mahādēviyamma

The main part of the referenced Shunya Sampadane pics up the story, and describes the Sampadane of Mōḷigayya and Mahādēviyamma. It also exemplifies the oneness of husband and wife.

Shunya Sampadane, in its prose section says that Mōḷige Mārayya who had been ruler of Kashmir, had come to Kalyana with his wife after abdicating his rule. At Kalyana he was performing worship of Jangama by following the vocation of a faggot gatherer. Jangamas who had already partaken sumptuous meal at Basavanna's house, then coming to Mārayya's cottage, further partook of the gruel prepared by Mahādēviyamma. Upon returning to Basavanna's place, the Jangamas spoke in extravagant praise of it.

One day, Basavanna, disguising as an ordinary devotee, visits their house. Bowing in reverence, Basavanna requests Mahādēviyamma to give him his meal as he was very hungry. Mahādēviyamma complies by arranging for his Linga worship, and after that, serving him her famous porridge. Basavanna is overjoyed by this gift of Grace.

Unknowing to Mahādēviyamma, Basavanna hides two containers with gold coins, behind the basin over which Ishtalinga is washed during worship.

Mōḷigayya comes home from work, and as usual, after taking a shower starts his Linga worship. He sees the gold coins, and from his wife, comes to know of a devotee's visit. He becomes enraged that their sense of dedicated work (kāyaka) and dedicated service (dāsōha) was offended by this bhakta (devotee), whom he instantly realizes to be none other than Basavanna.

After informing his wife, he goes to Basavanna's place, brings the Jangamas to his house for a meal. Mahādēviyamma feeds them the porridge. Mōḷigayya gives all the gold to Jangamas, and sends the Jangamas back to Basavanna.

Basavanna realizes his folly in daring to commiserate with the great Sharanas' poverty. **It is a mistake to think that Sharanas could suffer from poverty when they are living in tune with the Infinite and doing their dedicated work and service.** They are masters of Infinite wealth.

This situation puts Basavanna's bhakti (devotion) to a severe trial by Mōḷigayya. Thus repenting, Basavanna comes to Mōḷigayya's house with Chennabasavanna (Basavanna's intellectual and spiritually enlightened nephew), the great Shivayogi Siddharamayya, Haḍapada Appaṇṇa (a great Sharana and associate serving betel-nut and leaf) and others, and fully prostrating himself in humility, makes his submission and asks for forgiveness from Mōḷigayya.

Mōḷigayya would not be easily conciliated. He wonders how a bhakta of Basavanna's stature could forget himself and make such a mistake. Devotion done between forgetfulness and consciousness is not firm. In this context

Mōḷigayya has this vachana – vachana 11 on pages 84 and 85 in volume IV of Shunya Sampadane (1). It is as follows:

Devotion done self-consciously,
I say is oblivion's seed:
This way the ignorance and
Consciousness will never cease.
The nature of consciousness is
As light of lamp that is held up.
The consciousness of one who acts
In this self-conscious way,
Which knows and does not forget, is as
The steadiness of a lamp that is never lit,
O Niḥkaḷaṅkamallikārjuna.

The editors of volume IV of the referenced Shunya Sampadane (1), give explanation for the above vachana as follows: The idea of two kinds of consciousness is given in this vachana. The consciousness compared to the light of a lamp held up is the consciousness caught up between knowledge and ignorance. The light of the lamp is an eternal companion of darkness. The second kind of consciousness is that which transcends knowledge and forgetfulness. It is the self-effulgent light that is neither lighted nor extinguished.

Chennabasavanna condemns the action taken by Basavanna, and states that Basavanna was aware of the infinite powers latent in kāyaka, and that Mōḷigayya was no ordinary Sharana and Mōḷigayya's kāyaka was done in the utmost sincerity. Although Mōḷigayya does not approve of Basavanna's action, shows overflowing love and admiration for Basavanna.

Mōḷigayya makes it clear that **'bhakti should never be done for applause or admiration'.**

Siddharamayya also comes to the rescue, and then praises Mōḷigayya. There is complete reconciliation.

Mōḷigayya and Mahādēviyamma continue to lead the rigorous life of Sharanas. After the Sharanas leave the city of Kalyana following the revolution (it is described in the article 'Basavanna' in this book), Mōḷigayya and his wife continue to live at Kalyana. They spend their time in high spiritual discussions; their cottage becomes a mini Anubhava Mantapa.

After the Sharanas have dispersed away from Kalyana, Mōḷigayya exclaims to know his own path of attaining oneness. Vachana 19 on page 93 in volume IV of Shunya Sampadane is as follows:

When the place is lost and being sacked,
It is everyone for oneself!
Basavanna at Sangama,
Chennabasavanna at Uḷuve,
Prabhu at the Plantain-grove (Kadaḷi),
The rest of the saints have attained their
Salvation goal each at one's chosen spot.
Show me a path Niḥkaḷaṅkamallikārjuna!

The revolution/incident was the precipitating cause of the hurried departure from Kalyana of Basavanna and the Sharanas. Basavanna went to Kudala Sangama place. Chennabasavanna along with many Sharanas went to Ulavi. Allama Prabhudeva had already left Kalyana before this incident. He had gone to the plantain-grove (Kadaḷi) in the Shrishaila Mountains.

Mōḷigeya Mārayya and his wife Mahādēviyamma continue to live at Kalyana. They live to quite a ripe age at Kalyana.

Oneness of Husband and Wife

Mahādēviyamma had already shown a glimpse of this oneness of husband and wife situation when she had refused to stay behind at Kashmir and had accompanied her husband to Kalyana. She had indicated that her place is at the husband's side. Despite tremendous hardship of a long travel those days and difficult life at Kalyana without any material riches, she accompanied her husband to come to Kalyana.

After the Sharanas get dispersed away from Kalyana, Mōḷige Mārayya and his wife Mahādēviyamma spend their time in high spiritual discussions at Kalyana. Mōḷigayya is said to have a total of 818 available vachanas, and his wife Mahādēviyamma is said to have 69 vachanas (3).

The referenced Shunya Sampadane (1) depicts this Oneness discussion between husband

and wife in a total of 32 vachanas. In this context there are ten vachanas of Mōḷigayya and 22 vachanas of Mahādēviyamma. Some examples are given below.

Mōḷigayya expresses his eagerness for union with Linga. The way he expresses it, seems to imply duality. The vachana 19 on pages 92 and 93 in volume IV of Shunya Sampadane (1) is as follows:

In saying 'O', you are indeed a Formless one;
In saying 'Om' you are indeed
The personal Form;
In saying 'That Thou art', you took the
Maker's form as principle to save the world.

How long shall I keep up for You
This mission of a mortal man?
Is this a rigid covenant for me alone?
Tell me, Niḥkaḷaṅkamallikārjuna,
How many days must I perform this work
Imposed by you, peddling these
Faggots to the devotees' homes?

In the above vachana, it is said that 'O' stands for the Formless, 'Om' stands for the Formed, and 'That Thou art' stands for the manifested (1). The last of the three items *'tat-tvam-asi'* meaning *'That Thou art'* is from Chāndogya Upanishad (13). It is one of the great sayings of the Veda. It is repeated nine times with differing examples for the explanations. The complete message is as follows (13):

'That the Pure Being, the subtle essence of all, is the Self/Ātman of the whole universe. That is the True Reality. That is the Ātman. That you are'.

Mōḷigayya's statement 'How long shall I keep up for you this mission of a mortal man? And such...' implies duality.

Mahādēviyamma was surprised to hear such words from her husband. She seems to be more advanced spiritually than her husband. **She brings him up to the Reality - to the utter Oneness where there is none to ask and none to reply. To ask to be united with Reality implies duality, and so long as the duality persists, union is not possible.**

Mahādēviyamma's vachana 23 on page 97 in volume IV of Shunya Sampadane (1) is as follows:

What is this demand to be
In a state of unity with God?
This is not true piety.
Whatever you do, do you need
Another's counsel or comment?
What were you then before?
Tell me!

Know what this means
And understand yourself,

O Ennayyapriya Immaḍi
Niḥkaḷaṅkamallikārjuna!

Mahādēviyamma continues: Vachana 26 on pages 100 and 101 in volume IV of Shunya Sampadane (1) is as follows:

Light in hand,
Why should you complain it is dark?
When the alchemic stone is in your hand,
Why should you drudge for a wage?
With hunger satisfied, why should you
Bend under the hamper's load?

It is not proper for a devotee, who
Knows the temporal and the eterne,
To chatter about earth and Heaven,
When having gained the certitude
The shifting target has at last
Steadied itself and lodged in you,
You realize yourself the light of
The Absolute Void, in Ennayyapriya
Immaḍi Niḥkaḷaṅkamallikārjuna.

Mahādēviyamma in another vachana states that **'union' implies the union of two different things. But the ultimate union with the Reality is "union-less union".**

Vachana 29 on pages 103 and 104 in volume IV of Shunya Sampadane (1) is as follows:

When, with cessation of form
The formlessness remains, does
Formlessness desire to join form?

When form is lost in formlessness,
And this condition escapes compare,
The entire universe recedes.

When this condition is realized in your
Right will, your very body is Heaven.

This union with Linga is itself
The journey's end.
It is union with a thing
Transcending union.
You understand yourself, Ennayyapriya
Immaḍi Niḥkaḷaṅkamallikārjuna.

When one comes to the real knowledge and finds that one's actions flow from the Divine housed in one's body, and that the individual self is nothing but the Divine Self, then that one experiences the profound Truth and one's consciousness melts into Divine Consciousness.

In the following vachana, **Mahādēviyamma states that she is not something apart from her husband, she has become an integral part of his being. She has no separate existence to call her own.** Vachana 33 on pages108 and 109 in volume IV of Shunya Sampadane (1) is as follows:

Good Sir, has ever the head acted as body?
Good Sir, has ever the ear acted as eye?
Good Sir, has ever the nose acted as mouth?
Tell me, good Sir, how,
Motherless, can children come?

Why should you care to know the
Thinking of your servant maid?
You think the kite's tail stands in need
Of supplementary string?

My heart has clung to you, in Ennayyapriya
Immaḍi Niḥkaḷaṅkamallikārjuna.

It is stated that Mahādēviyamma holds up an ideal of womanhood and that of the mystic union of two beings living on the same plane of spiritual experience (1).

In the following vachana, Mōḷige Mārayya remarks that may be because she is with him in his practice and piety that he has no sense of difference between them two. Vachana 35 on page 110 in volume IV of Shunya Sampadane (1) is as follows:

Does the foot walk without the head?
Does the mouth eat without the stomach?
What chance is there for hands and
Legs in the absence of the soul?
The growth of your devotion is
My way of truth: that is sure,
O Niḥkaḷaṅkamallikārjuna!

Mahādēviyamma responds by explaining that there is no otherness or difference between the Absolute Linga and him. Vachana 37 on pages 112 and 113 in volume IV of Shunya Sampadane (1) is as follows:

Through ignorance that

It has become a symbol for the union,
Through ignorance that
It has become awareness for the Self,
Your spirit has succumbed to the
Control of Heaven's strings!
Alas, you have been like
A blind man with a jewel in his hand!
Like cripple with weapon in his hand!

When you have firmly understood
The disembodied state, there is no bother
About this dual sense which says
There is other to be merged into.

Wherever you stand, there is true union;
Where your mind is clear,
There is the disembodied state.
There is no One and Other in Ennayyapriya
Immaḍi Niḥkaḷaṅkamallikārjuna.

It is said that this vachana describes the state of a Sharana who lives in the highest experience. When Sharana is completely aware of his identity with the Self, he has no individualized existence that is limited by body, vital breath, and such.

Then in vachana 40 on pages 115 and 116 in volume IV of Shunya Sampadane (1), Mahādēviyamma describes the various stages through which a seeker has to go through to finally attain the Absolute One. The description in the vachana is as follows:

- First, one has to recognize the real teacher, a Guru, in one's spiritual path. Guru reveals to the one, the Divine enshrined in one's heart, and puts Ishtalinga the representation of the inner Divine on to one's palm.
- Second, when one comes to the realization of the Linga the Divine - which can occur only after eliminating any hatred, enmity and violence, and purging all the evil desires and inclinations such as lust, anger, greed, infatuation, ego and jealousy - one has to express that Divine in practice; the Divine expressions are Love, Knowledge, Power, Bliss and Peace.
- Third, when the Divine is firmly established in both knowledge and action, one attains the Supreme Knowledge that is Jangama.
- Then the six-fold hierarchy, the Shatsthala, is a matter of living experience; the time comes when all the varied love, knowledge, discipline and action consummate into realization of the Absolute.

In the following vachana, **Mahādēviyamma reiterates the concept that husband and wife are not two but one. Further, she states that even while in this duality of I and You, one should get to disembodied state in the Linga which pervades one's being.** She suggests that Mōḷigayya, in the deepest of his being, is in that very state. Vachana 42 on pages 117 and 118 in volume IV of Shunya Sampadane (1) is as follows:

As long as there is body,
There is worship of Linga;
As long as there is self,
There is this state of Consciousness;
To say you are man,
I am wife – is seed of duality.

Even when there is this I and you,
You need to be in a disembodied state
In Aṅga's Liṅga, O Ennayyapriya
Immaḍi Niḥkaḷaṅkamallikārjuna.

Mahādēviyamma then describes their unitive experience through **Shaṭsthala**. Vachana 46 on pages 121 and 122 in volume IV of Shunya Sampadane (1) is as follows:

Where heart and intellect are whole,
There is the Bhaktasthala;
Where there is sense of clean and unclean,
There is Maheshvarasthala;
Where there is sense of knowledge and
Ignorance, there is Prasadisthala;
Where the sense of union of the two
Is rooted out, there is Pranalingisthala;
Where body is dead and still to censure
And to praise, there is Sharanasthala;
Where, above all difference, you are
Conscious of the links between these
Five-fold differences, and the knower
And the known symbol become one,
There is Aikyasthala.

That, my lord, is the six-fold hierarchy

Shatsthala of you and me.
There is no separation there;
It is like the joy of you and me
Made one in love.

Give this your careful thought, pray.
No more the stud-bull roving here and there!
Even as you say so,
You must pass into the Void, Ennayyapriya
Immaḍi Niḥkaḷaṅkamallikārjuna!

The above vachana further asserts that there is no separation between them two; it is them two made one in love.

Mahādēviyamma plays a magnificent role in shaping the spiritual life of Mōḷige Mārayya. Mōḷigayya understands the true significance of the consubstantial union – the union-less union. He acknowledges the wisdom of his wife, and becomes one with his own Self; and then Mahādēviyamma too, with him and the Absolute.

There are 49 vachanas in this thirteenth chapter, bringing the subtotal to 887 vachanas.

Chapter 14

NULIYA CHANDAYYA'S SAMPĀDANE

In the opening verse at the beginning of this fourteenth chapter, the composer Gūḷūra Siddhavīraṇārya says that he gladly tells the story of an eminent Sharana by name Nuliya Chandayya who had an illustrious life on earth, and had compelled his Linga to render well the dedicated work.

Chandayya was a rope maker. He strictly followed the principles of dedicated labor Kāyaka. He believed that everyone including Guru, Linga and Jangama is not exempt from Kāyaka. He also believed that devotion to Jangama is devotion to Linga; Jangama worship is Linga worship; fulfillment in Jangama is fulfillment in Linga; service to Jangama is the farthest reach; and that wherever all actions are done to Jangama there the mind would be absorbed. To him the service of Jangama was an end.

One day on his customary work, having cut the grass, was tying up the grass into trusses to make ropes. His Ishtalinga, as if to test whether his great dedication to Jangama was real or not, slipped and fell into the water. Chandayya thought to himself, 'if the Linga wanted Jangama-service, it would comeback itself'. He did not want to interrupt his dedicated work. He did not pick up the Linga; he was walking away without picking it up.

Maḍivāḷayya (Maḍivāḷayya's Sampadane is in chapter nine) was washing clothes nearby. He asked Chandayya why he shut the door on Linga. Chandayya answered that Jangama service is more important, and as long as Jangama service is done, nothing divides him from the Linga.

Maḍivāḷayya then tells him that even Guru and Jangama have to worship Linga; without Linga there is no meaning in Jangama, and that Chandayya should know that he must have Linga on himself and it is the only way to know the Divine.

Chandayya responds by saying - to have a pure heart is tantamount to Guru's worship; to have a pure consciousness is as good as worship of Linga; to be pure in the three senses, and to be purged clean of the triple impurity is worship of Jangama.

Maḍivāḷayya then says: 'because you have attained to knowledge, that does not mean that you should give up activity; each deed that is done must keep both gaze and heart upon worship of Linga; that is the union with the Divine'.

Chandayya's response – worship of Linga needs sixteen-fold service, and while you do it, there is no more work!

Maḍivāḷayya responds – one should not show the slightest lack in keeping of a vow; virtue demands its proper energy; one must do one's worship however short the time.

Chandayya then says a vow does not know the beginning, middle or the end; it is a certain doubt if having let go one, you yet cling to another!

Maḍivāḷayya asks – can there be service of Jangama without Linga? Linga is the body of Jangama; can there be any life without body? After all functions of your work have turned to Linga, can there be still substantial difference?

Chandayya answers – The Ishṭa is Guru's dependency; both Guru and Ishṭa are contained in Jangama for both are dependent on Jangama. Then he bows to Maḍivāḷayya, and taking Linga with him, goes home.

Addressing his Liṅga, Chandayya goes over the details for not falling for greed:

- One's mind must not be ruffled with whatever income comes from work.
- There must be harmony between the wages you have asked and your habitual wage.
- If you grasp money, coveting gold in your greed and waving the wages of your vow, the service you have rendered will come to nothing.
- Do not walk into the noose of the greed.

- The irksome work such as to beg and bring from whomsoever by fretting, worrying, binding, and/or injuring, in the name of service to Jaṅgama, is not fit as an offering to Liṅga.
- A kare leaf (kare leaf is used during Liṅga worship) that comes from dedicated work is worthy to be offered to Liṅga, but not the one that comes of covetousness.
- Therefore, the daily wage that comes of dedicated work, righteous and pure, is consecrated food to Liṅga.

Maḍivāḷayya and Chandayya then go to Anubhava Mantapa to discuss the issue of Ishtalinga further.

Chandayya, bowing down to all the Sharanas on the occasion, relates the manner of his work, the real meaning of his service, and the mode of his faith so as to make it known to all the Sharanas there. Then he states: Guru gives Ishtalinga to the disciple; the disciple, in obedience to the Guru's word, worships the Linga; for this the disciple goes to heaven as a reward; going to heaven does not stop the cycle of births and deaths; complete surrender to Jangama-Linga is the surest and easiest way to attain complete liberation from the cycle of births and deaths.

Prabhudeva responds by stating that after one has known the Linga, it must not be given up; if one worships in loyalty to Linga, one must possess a Sign. Chandayya responds by saying if you serve Guru, there is happiness in this world; if you serve Linga, there is happiness in the next world; if you serve Jangama, the dual sense of this and next worlds is gone.

Prabhudeva: as long as you have the body, worship of Linga is to be done; even when the body ceases to be, the sense of Linga must persist. Chandayya: worshippers of Guru cannot know Linga, and worshippers of Linga cannot know Jangama, whereas the service of Jangama entails cessation of duality.

Prabhudeva brings a simile to explain that knowledge and experience of threefold Linga is essential to come to the Unitive knowledge of Linga which has assumed the three-fold form, and that Ishtalinga is indispensable for living an integral divine life. Chandayya: whether be Guru, Linga or Jangama, only dedicated work (Kāyaka) can pluck off the bonds; no one can escape the law of Kāyaka.

Prabhudeva then states – one must stay constantly in the observations and vows that one has taken; and if one keeps a clear heart in these vows and observations which the person practices every day, one is not strange or different from Guheshvara-Linga.

Then Chandayya submits that his service consisting of his devotion, action, knowledge and conduct is dear to Basavanna. Thus Prabhudeva asks Basavanna, that he being the prime

Preceptor, he should make it clear to Chandayya. But Basavanna tells Prabhudeva to ask Chennabasavanna. Prabhudeva then asks Chennabasavanna to explain the essence of integral Linga to Chandayya.

Accordingly Chennabasavanna explains: Guru's grace is Linga, and Linga's grace is Jangama; that is the external practice. The right knowledge of the inner being is Jangama; when Jangama is seen in motion, its right acts are Linga; and the oneness of the two is Guru. Therefore, when the triple Linga is united with triple anga, that is the service of Jangama, without which there is no content for Linga. Unless the Linga is on the body, Jangama will not accept service. Therefore, to stand on one, abandoning the other, is as soul without the body, as light without a lamp; there is no devotion if one aspect is not there. The body of Jangama is the Linga with the form, Prabhudeva!

Prabhudeva rightly says to Chandayya 'listen to Chennabasavanna's glorious words'. Vachana 48 on page 190 in volume IV of Shunya Sampadane (1) is as follows:

Good deeds are Linga, and
Their proper understanding is Jangama.
Anga is Linga, its energy is Jangama.
Service of Jangama is Linga,
He who accepts it is Jangama.
You live, O Chandayya,
By the grace of Chennabasavanna

Who has reported this
Just as Maḍivāḷa does his work,
So that Guheshvara's Sharanas are satisfied.

Anga is Linga; its energy is Jangama; service to Jangama is Linga; one who accepts it is Jangama.

Chandayya signifies his agreement with the statements, and holding his Ishtalinga tells Prabhudeva the enlightenment of Sharana has come to him.

There are 49 vachanas in this fourteenth chapter; the subtotal comes to 936 vachanas.

Chapter 15

GHAṬṬIVĀḶAYYA'S SAMPĀDANE

Ghaṭṭivāḷayya, one of the great Sharanas of the twelfth century, taught everyone a lesson with regard to Jangama, the Community Order, and the Linga.

Editors of volume IV of Shunya Sampadane give this information (1): Muddaṇṇa, as he was known before he came to Kalyana, followed the profession of dancer/actor, and he was highly accomplished in the act of playing mrudaṅga (a type of double sided drum). He was a strong-willed person, being candid and forthright even when it involved the highest in society. Because of his courage and unshakable determination, he was called Ghaṭṭivāḷayya which means a tough bold person. His professional performance earned his livelihood and helped him serve the Sharanas.

One day, after having come to Kalyana he went to Basavanna's courtyard where he observed a crowd of people who were wearing Jangama garb, and who upon hearing the announcement that the food was ready, competitively rushed to get their meal. He was shocked and amused at the same time. This set him off on an analysis of them Jangamas.

In the first ten consecutive vachanas in this chapter, Ghaṭṭivāḷayya describes his analysis:

- A true Jangama is a moving God.
- The Jangama-Linga's garb should not be a means for sustenance or satisfaction of the body.
- Jangama should accept only when the offering is done with love and devotion.
- Jangama should never hanker after women, land and gold/wealth.
- Jangama is not tainted by any defects in the qualities.

After stating that, Ghaṭṭivāḷayya denounces and derides the crowd's behavior, and even questions the sincerity of Basavanna's piety.

The crowd offended by this, calls him names, and attacks and manhandles him. This does not stop Ghaṭṭivāḷayya. He continues to ridicule them. This row draws many of the Sharanas including Prabhudeva to the spot.

Prabhudeva, intervening, requests Ghaṭṭivāḷayya not to disparage the Community of the Jangama Order.

Ghaṭṭivāḷayya replies:

- The Order should be like an 'ocean'; it should not be upset whenever its defects and shortcomings are pointed out.
- The Community should accept constructive criticism gladly, and should try it's best for the growth and betterment of the individuals of which it is composed of.

The crowd, not satisfied, forcibly takes away Ghaṭṭivāḷayya's Ishtalinga from him. This is an extreme punishment for a Veerashaiva. Ghaṭṭivāḷayya unruffled by this, openly defies the convention. He declares in vachana 28 on pages 226 and 227 in volume IV of Shunya Sampadane:

That which gets worshipped on this earth
In static form is Shiva-Linga;

That which gets worshipped on this earth
In the dynamic form is Ishtalinga;

That which, abiding eternally
Upon the point of Consciousness,
Gets worshipped is Veerashaiva-Linga.

In ignorance of the source and substance
Of these three aspects of Linga,
Alas, they went astray!
Whom else shall I tell this?
Chikkayyapriya Siddhaliṅga,
I say, is not in such!

'Shiva-Linga is the one that is worshipped in a static form at a temple on earth. Ishtalinga is the one that is worshipped in the dynamic form on earth. But that, abiding within, eternally upon the point of Consciousness, and gets worshipped internally, is the Veerashaiva-Linga'.

He places a huge round stone at the gate blocking it, and ties a rope to the stone and to his neck. For him the nearest stone could serve as Ishtalinga.

All the great Sharanas including Prabhudeva, Basavanna, Chennabasavanna, and Siddharamayya witness what was going on. They acclaim that Ghaṭṭivāḷayya is a true devotee, a great yogi, and a real practitioner of the Veerashaiva discipline; and that he is the one who could see no difference between the Ishtalinga and a big wayside stone.

The great Sharanas, particularly Chennabasavanna, appear ready to revise their opinion with regard to wearing the Ishtalinga. In the past when Prabhudeva had brought with him, an already well-established great Shivayogi Siddharamayya, to the city of Kalyana, the Sharanas were reluctant to admit Siddharamayya because he was not wearing Ishtalinga. When Nuliya Chandayya refused to take back the Ishtalinga that had fallen off of him while he was intensely engaged in his kāyaka of cutting grass to make ropes, the same Sharanas had convinced him about the necessity of wearing it all the time. Now they seem to make an exception. Ghaṭṭivāḷayya is considered as a Liṅgavanta, 'the one possessed of Linga', and does not need the Ishtalinga. Whatever Ghaṭṭivāḷayya wears turns into Linga; for him there is nothing that is not Linga.

Ghaṭṭivāḷayya, the Liṅgavanta, taught everyone a lesson with regard to Jangama, the Community Order, and Linga. His mission being accomplished, he attained oneness with Shunya.

There are 67 vachanas with songs in this fifteenth chapter. The subtotal comes to 1,003 vachanas.

Chapter 16

MAHĀDĒVIYAKKA'S SAMPĀDANE

Mahādēviyakka is more popularly known as Akka Mahadevi. In the vachanas, Akka Mahādēvi is usually referred to as Mahadeviyakka. Sometimes, the name of Akka Mahadevi is written as Akkamahādēvi. It is all one and the same.

The twelfth century Sharaṇas considered every one, whether a man or a woman, to be the spiritual spouse of the Supreme Divine. That meant that the Sharana is a dedicated wife serving the Supreme Divine. Life of *Sharaṇe* Mahadeviyakka most closely depicts the life of a spiritual spouse.

The meaning of the Kannada word 'Sharaṇa' is 'to surrender'. The Kannada word 'Sharaṇa' is masculine and it is applicable to a man, whereas the word 'Sharaṇe' is feminine and it is applicable to a woman. But, the term Sharana is used in general for both men and women.

Akka Mahādēvi

The editors of volume IV of Shunya Sampadane give the following information about Mahadeviyakka (1):

Mahadeviyakka was born at Uḍutaḍi, a village about 35 miles from Shivamogga in the Karnataka State, India. Her parents Sumati and

Nirmala were very much influenced by the Sharana way of life. Mahadeviyakka received Veerashaiva initiation at an early age by a spiritual Guru. This initiation ceremony, apparently meant to her that her Guru bound her irrevocably in wedlock to the Supreme Divine Chenna-Mallikarjuna.

Mahadeviyakka grew to be a beautiful teenage girl. One day when she was about sixteen years of age, she was watching the King Kaushika and his retinue pass by. The king happened to see her and was captivated by her beauty. Upon his return to his palace, he sent his minister to the house of Mahadeviyakka's parents to seek the consent to marry Mahadeviyakka. But her parents refused without any hesitation.

This put Mahadeviyakka at a dilemma – death of her parents in the hands of the king, or to marry a non-Veerashaiva king. To resolve this situation, noting that the king would agree to any terms to marry her, got a commitment from him that he would wear a Linga.

But, after the marriage, the king did not convert and did not wear the Linga. This precipitated an event where Mahadeviyakka shed everything including her clothes, and left the village naked. It stunned the king and everyone else.

Mahadeviyakka travelled for many months to the city of Kalyana where she obtained her spiritual enlightenment.

After spending some time with the Sharanas at Kalyana and acquiring spiritual wisdom, she left Kalyana to go to Shrishaila. Shrishaila is about 250 miles from Kalyana. That journey those days was much too difficult. Guided by Allama Prabhudeva's direction, Mahadeviyakka makes her way to Mount Shrishaila.

Mahadeviyakka sets up camp at Mount Shrishaila, and spends some more time there. She attains unitive state Shunya at a very young age of 25 years.

Mahadeviyakka has authored 354 vachanas that are available (3). Her vachana signature is Chenna-Mallikarjuna. It is said that her vachanas are rich in lyrical quality and high thinking. It is also said that the vachanas she sang on the way to Shrishaila and at Shrishaila are, apart from exquisite lyrical beauty, gems of mystic utterance.

According to the referenced Shunya Sampadane (1) Mahadeviyakka has also authored the following works:

1. Yōgāṅga Trividhi
2. Shrestha Vachana
3. Padagaḷu
4. Akkagaḷa Pīṭhike.

Ganaka Vachana Samputa reference (3) has all the 354 Kannada vachanas of Mahadeviyakka. Most of these vachanas have been translated to English in that reference.

Sampadane of Akka Mahādēvi

Spiritual achievement at the age of sixteen

The author of the fourth version of Shunya Sampadane, Gūḷūra Siddhavīraṇārya, in the prose section at the beginning, gives an outline of Mahadeviyakka's life and spiritual achievement. This achievement is said to be at the age of sixteen when she comes to the city of Kalyana. It is described in the referenced Shunya Sampadane (1). Some of the descriptions are as follows:

She refused to touch anyone who would not wear the Linga; she shed all sense of the body and became integrally united with the Linga; she was in her prime of sixteen; she possessed a splendid beauty and charm; she made a sacrifice of all her senses to the consciousness; wore only the sky for her garment and covered herself with a cloak of her hair; radiated complete indifference to the world; showered the essence of compassion; acquired a steady wisdom; and such.

It is said that, here, nakedness or nudity is not just the baring the body of clothes, but it also means the renunciation of all worldly ties (1).

In one of her vachanas, Mahadeviyakka describes her achievement as to how she reduced her lust to ashes. The vachana has a Hindu mythological story which is not applicable to the Sharanas. The story is described below. Vachana 2 on page 284 of volume IV of Shunya Sampadane (1) is as follows:

Through the joy of Linga
I achieved the body's defeat;
By way of knowledge
I achieved defeat of mind;
Through God-experience
I achieved defeat of soul;
Donning the Light as garment
I subdued the darkness of the senses.
Look at the ashes I have worn when
Kama burnt who shows himself to you
Within the outer gloss of youth!
If Chenna-Mallikārjuna after slaying Kāma
Let him live as the heart-born,
I erased the writing on the
Head of the heart-born!

According to the Hindu beliefs, *Kāma* is the divinity of love and lust. The legendary story is that, while Shiva was meditating intensely, Kama fires his arrow of Love unto Shiva in order to end Shiva's meditation so that Shiva would involve in love making with his wife Parvathi to produce an offspring. This was necessary, as the legendary story goes, because only Shiva's son could destroy the terrorizing demon Tarakasura. Upon Kama's flower arrow touching its intended target, Shiva opens his third eye on his forehead and burns Kama to ashes. However, upon Parvathi's request, Shiva lets Kama live without a body – thus Kama is known as *'Anaṅga'* which means *'bodiless'*. In the above vachana, Mahadeviyakka uses the term 'heart-born' for the body-less Kama. The rest of the Mythological story in simple terms is that, Shiva-Parvathi union is consummated, son Karthikeya is born, and Karthikeya defeats the terrorizing demon Tarakasura.

This mythological story is from the Puranas. The story is in several Puranas with some differences. It is not applicable to the Sharanas. But here, Mahadeviyakka uses it to describe how she got rid of lust.

Arrival at Kalyana

In Shunya Sampadane (1), the author Gūḷūra Siddhavīraṇārya in its prose section says something like this: As Mahadeviyakka was coming to Kalyana, Basavanna informs Prabhudeva *'...Akka Mahadevi, having in her austerity rendered herself nude in defiance to lust, is coming'.* Then Prabhudeva, in order to show to all the Sharanas what a lust-slayer she is, sends Kinnarayya to her.

Out of a spirit of devotion, Kinnarayya tests Mahadeviyakka who shows him how she had reduced lust to ashes in the fire of intuitional knowledge and says to him *'to me who have burnt lust to ashes, Linga is husband, and you a brother'.*

After taking leave of Kinnarayya, Mahadeviyakka walks towards the city of Kalyana.

Mahadeviyakka describes who cannot, and who can, enter the holy city of Kalyāṇa. Vachana 4 on pages 286 and 287 in volume IV of Shunya Sampadane (1), is as follows:

Not anyone can go, can go, can go
To Kalyana; it cannot be done!
Unless you shed all greed and lust,
You cannot go Kalyana way.
Unless you are pure within and without,
You cannot go Kalyana way.
Unless you pluck away your sense of self,
You cannot go Kalyana way.

Because I have cleansed my inner self
Because I have loved Chenna-Mallikārjuna,
And cancelled the shame of the dual sense,
I have seen Kalyāṇa.
Therefore I say and say again,
Hail, O hail!

So saying, Mahadeviyakka enters the city of Kalyana. She extols the glory of Basavanna as she walks along. She then enters Basavanna's place and sees the holy person of Basavanna amidst innumerable great Sharanas, Prabhudeva chief among them. When Mahadeviyakka upon meeting Basavanna's holy feet, having done obeisance to him, and standing in front of him with folded hands, Basavanna presents her to Prabhudeva, saying *'...behold the majesty of Mahadeviyakka'.* (1).

Inquisition of Mahadeviyakka

When a sixteen year old nude woman comes to the sacred spiritual, religious and social academy (Anubhava Mantapa), despite what she has accomplished by then, further inquiry is deemed necessary particularly to assess how far she has advanced in her spiritually.

Allama Prabhudeva who was the chief among the Sharanas at the Anubhava Mantapa carries out this inquisition of Mahadeviyakka.

Prabhudeva puts the questions in his vachanas. These vachanas and the response vachanas of Mahadeviyakka are in the Shunya Sampadane reference (1) on pages 292 through 318 of volume IV. It is said that Prabhudeva makes Mahadeviyakka speak out of joy of her mystic experience.

Prabhudeva asks her to come and sit, and asks her the reason why she has come there in the lusty bloom of youth and what her husband's identity is.

Mahadeviyakka reveals her husband's identity in three vachanas. She describes her symbolic wedding to the Absolute Devine. She uses the terms Hara, Chenna-Mallikarjuna, and also Linga for the Absolute Divine.

In the first of the three vachanas, Mahadeviyakka states that she made penance for endless time to get the attention of the Divine, so she may be wedded to the Divine Chenna-Mallikarjuna. It is said that as she advances in her yogic practices she experiences brilliant colors and such, symbolizing the performance of her marriage-rite.

In the second vachana, Mahadeviyakka describes the decorations at the wedding. These decorations are symbolic.

In the third vachana, Mahadeviyakka describes the conductance of the wedding. Kinsman was the Guru to officiate, Linga was the bridegroom and she was the bride; innumerable saints were her parents, they gave her away to a fitting groom. Therefore, Chenna-Mallikarjuna is her lord and no other person in the world is her husband.

Prabhudeva remarks whether it is true that she laid blame on king Kaushika for not wearing the Linga and left him; and that as she came there in a nude state with her hair as a screen, her self-consciousness is not yet shed because she wears her hair to cover her form.

Mahadeviyakka responds – once the heart is purified, what does it matter what body it is that Chenna-Mallikarjuna loves?

After this response from her, an intense discussion takes place.

Prabhudeva asks – 'What does it mean that God loves you and you love God? If your spirit is pure, why do you cloak yourself in hair? The shame that lurks within your heart shows outside.'

Mahadeviyakka answers – She covers herself because the sight of seals of love may hurt others; there is no harm in that; and not to tease her who is in Chenna-Mallikarjuna, the God of gods.

Unless the fruit is ripe within,
The outer peel will never lose its gloss.
I covered myself with this intent:
Lest sight of seals of love should do you hurt.
Is any harm in this?
Do not tease me who am in
Chenna-Mallikārjuna, God of gods.

Prabhudeva then asks what is the point of whether Mahadeviyakka is in God or God is in her, and asks when she subdued the god of love.

Sharana Philosophy is that, although God encompasses everything including the Self, and that, technically everything is in God, still **God is said to be within you, and not the other way around. Once one merges in the Absolute, there is no individual-self in God. One has become God itself. Therefore, the saying that 'you are in God' cannot arise.**

Mahadeviyakka replies that she made her home within Chenna-Mallikarjuna, but there is no trace of her former body there.

For one who, like a burnt-up corpse,
Like puppet with a broken string,
Like tank whose water has dried up,

Like a burnt cord, has made her house
Within Chenna-Mallikārjuna's body,
Is there still her former body's trace?

Mahadeviyakka continues her response stating that she loves the beautiful One, the formless One who is beyond death and dissolution, the fearless, and the dauntless, and that Chenna-Mallikarjuna is her husband and no other.

O Sir, I love the beautiful One,
The formless One who is
Beyond death or dissolution;
I love the beautiful One, the fearless,
The dauntless One who is past birth.
Chenna-Mallikārjuna is my husband,
All other husbands in the world
Are naught to me!

Prabhudeva is not satisfied with that answer. He says how can there be marriage between the form and formlessness; so long as there is the natural taint of body and the senses, one cannot reach the Divine. Once one has understood the body, the mind is to be purified; when the mind is understood, the senses are to be purified; **until the body, mind and senses are made pure and tranquil, and turned Linga-ward, one cannot reach the Divine.**

It is said that to make the body, mind and senses pure, it is necessary to analyze, know and understand their nature and qualities, and then empty them of all their creaturely qualities. Once the body, mind and the senses are purified and thus fit for offering, they are offered to the Divine; that is how one reaches and knows the Divine.

Mahadeviyakka responds – Those who are loved by Chenna-Mallikārjuna do not have a body. Her body was purified by taking what is left from true devotees; mind was purified by remembering innumerable ones; eyes were purified by seeing all the ancient ones; ears were purified by listening to their praises; and the wheel of birth has ceased by worshipping Chenna-Mallikārjuna with all her heart.

By taking leftovers from true devotees,
My body is purified;
By remembering the countless ones,
My mind is purified;
By seeing all the ancient ones,
My eyes are purified;
By listening to their praise,
My ears are purified.
Hear me, O Father Linga,
This feeling has become my life.
Worshipping Thee with all my heart,
My wheel of births has ceased,
O Chenna-Mallikārjuna!

Mahadeviyakka continues her response in another vachana saying that - By seeing Basavanna's feet her body has become as naught; seeing Chennabasavanna's feet her life too has become a void; and bowing to Prabhudeva's holy feet, her awareness has come to her. As she has earned the mercy of Chenna-Mallikārjuna's Sharanas, there is nothing more for her.

Prabhudeva then says, mere purity of body, life and will does not mean that Linga is firm, and that it will lead to ultimate Reality; higher spiritual experience may be essential for that.

Mahadeviyakka says she has gone beyond purity in all parts of her being; as Linga is firmly established in all these, they are all of Linga. The Absolute has become the thought of her whole mind.

Within my body there is a disembodied state;
Within my life there is Transcending life;
Within my will there is a will-less-ness.
The Absolute has become the thought
Of my whole mind.
Because you, seeing my head and breasts,
Befriended me, I now belong to
Chenna-Mallikārjuna's grace.

Prabhudeva responds by saying that there is no 'Absolute' other than one's own 'Self'; to speak of merging in the Absolute is a flaw.

This is a finer point. **It is not just merging in the Absolute, it is becoming the Absolute itself – The Absolute and the Self is one and the same.**

Mahadeviyakka responds by saying that the holy Guru has made her body to melt into formlessness; she lost her consciousness the moment she merged in her Lord Chenna-Mallikarjuna.

Sir, is there a difference between
Solidified and liquid clarified butter?
A difference between lamp and light?
Between the body and soul?
Because the holy Guru has proved
My body to be a charm,
There is no difference between
The partite and the Non-partite.
I have lost my consciousness the moment
I merged in Chenna-Mallikārjuna Dēva,
Why do you make me speak, O Prabhu?

Prabhudeva is still not satisfied with her answer. It is said that if she is aware of the identity of Consciousness, then the individual consciousness is still there. When the 'I' itself is the Supreme Consciousness, there emerges the state with no individual consciousness, which she might not have attained. **Once one has attained the Absolute state, there is no individual consciousness.**

Mahadeviyakka describes the process by which she attained to the highest spiritual experience where she no longer knows what the 'I' is or where: 'While still in body's company, I have become Linga's companion, and while in Linga's company, I am body's companion; transcending the company of both, I have attained to peace; after forgetting this cluster of words, what if one lives an integral life? Once I am joined to Lord Chenna-Mallikarjuna, I do not recognize myself as anything'.

While still in body's company,
I have become Linga's companion;
While in Linga's company,
I am body's companion.
Transcending the company of both,
I have attained to peace.
After forgetting the cluster of words,
What if one lives an integral life?
Once I am joined to
Chenna-Mallikarjuna Deva,
I do not recognize myself as anything.

Now Prabhudeva is satisfied with Mahadeviyakka's answer. Prabhudeva recognizes that Mahadeviyakka is spiritually advanced. He then praises her. This is vachana 41 on pages 316 and 317 in volume IV of Shunya Sampadane (1) is as follows:

The body is a woman's form;
The mind, one with the spirit of the Thing.
Yet you come down here
Because you had a reason to come,
And this you have done!
Akka, you have transcended the sense
Of two in Guheshvara-Linga, sister mine.

Then, a brief inquiry of Mahadeviyakka by Basavanna begins.

Inquiry by Basavanna

Basavanna then tests Mahadeviyakka's spirituality briefly, and asserts his own comments.

Basavanna, in his vachana, says 'If you have achieved union with Linga while in body, Shiva will tease you by blocking up your further way; Shiva will make you toil and toss in desire of lust; Shiva in disgust will flee from the body far away. Listen to me, Shiva loves union where the woman becomes a man; if you would unite yourself with Shiva, you must without a sense of difference be a valiant man; that is so!'

Mahadeviyakka responds to the above question and comment of Basavanna in two vachanas.

In the first of her two vachanas of response, Mahadeviyakka says something like 'a woman though in name, I am the masculine principle'. Vachana 44 on pages 319 and 320 in volume IV of Shunya Sampadane (1) is like this:

Through your grace, Sir, Basavanna,
I have conquered lust;
Through your grace, Sir, Basavanna,
I will make captive of the holder of the moon;
Through your grace, you see, Basavanna,
A woman though in name, I am, if you
Consider well, the masculine principle.
And if I have ensnared
Chenna-Mallikārjuna's intemperate love,

And, being one with him,
Transcending the two,
Have quite forgot myself, it is through
Your grace, Basavanna, Sir!

In the above vachana, holder of the moon refers to Shiva who is adorned with the Moon on his crown/head. This is a Shaiva concept of Shiva; it is not a Sharana concept.

In the second vachana of response to Basavanna, Mahadeviyakka says something like 'After transcending the body's nature and shedding all taste of difference, and learning the taste of Linga, I have killed Chenna-Mallikarjuna and died myself'. This statement is further explained below. Vachana 45 on page 321 in volume IV of Shunya Sampadane (1) is something like this:

If you would consider thoughtfully, it is body;
But after I have transcended body's nature,
I have become your body;
And after I have shed all taste of difference
And learned the taste of Linga, it means
I have killed Chenna-Mallikarjuna
And died myself.

It is to be noted that the Absolute Divine which is also the one's own Self, is eternal. It can neither be killed nor does it die. In the comments and notes section of Shunya Sampadane (1), the editors of volume IV of the reference, explain what Mahadeviyakka means when she states 'I have killed Chenna-Mallikarjuna and died myself'. It is as follows:

'Such statements indeed seem to be very bold, but they reflect the highest state of spiritual experience in which there is no more God or the devotee. It may be incidentally remarked that such a state is called Bayalu or Shunya, the Void, and more, it is also experienced as Sarva-Shunya or Nisshunya. In a sense it may be described as Experience beyond all states'.

Basavanna responds: 'He is not one to perish or remain; He does not know what dissolution is; He is exempt from the nature of time and duality. Tell me, can you win, while laboring in this tremor of heat, the Silent One?'

Mahadeviyakka replies 'Joining body, mind, will, and knowledge in Linga, and suspending action and going beyond inaction, I have attained union with the ultimate Linga; having dissolved myself in Chenna-Mallikarjuna, I have dissolved the Absolute called Linga within myself, mark that Sangana Basavanna!' Vachana 47 on pages 322 and 323 in volume IV of Shunya Sampadane (1) is as follows:

Becoming Body in body,
I have joined Body to Linga;
Becoming Mind in mind,
I have joined Mind to Linga;
Becoming Will in will,

I have joined Will to Linga;
Becoming Knowledge in knowledge,
I have joined Knowledge to Linga.

Suspending action and going beyond
Inaction, I have attained
Union with the ultimate Linga;
Suspending the I, erasing the Thou,
Having dissolved myself in
Chenna-Mallikarjuna, I have dissolved
The Absolute called Linga within myself;
Mark that, Sangana Basavanna!

Basavanna being satisfied with the answer, praises Mahadeviyakka. Vachana 48 on pages 323 and 324 in volume IV of Shunya Sampadane (1) is as follows:

Behold the body of the woman-child,
O ancients!
Behold the innocent form, O ancients!
Behold her who lives by means of chastity,
In self-forgetfulness, wearers of the Linga!
Establishing herself within her Self,
The life she lives without infringement of
Her pledge has come to be,
In Kudala Sangama Deva
For our Mahadeviyakka!

Mahadeviyakka responds in two vachanas, and praises Basavanna. Vachana 49 on pages 324 and 325 in volume IV of Shunya Sampadane (1) is as follows:

Beholding your body's discipline, I

Accomplished union with Linga, Basavanna!
Beholding the wisdom of your mind, I have
Made contact with Jangama, Basavanna!
Perceiving your real piety,
I have attained Reality, Basavanna!
Because by naming Chenna-Mallikarjuna,
You have become my Guru,
There is no I for me, Basavanna!

Mahadeviyakka continues her praise of Basavanna. Vachana 50 on pages 325 and 326 in volume IV of Shunya Sampadane (1) is as follows:

He manifested Discipline within the body,
And explained the Discipline to be Linga;
Established Consciousness within the breath,
And showed this
Consciousness to be Jangama.
Sangana Basavanna, father who bore
Chenna-Mallikarjuna
Explained this process to me, Sir.

Then there is Mahadeviyakka's vachana where she extols Basavanna. In that vachana, she says that Basavanna, after incorporating the fifty-two principles, moved around to teach the path of Veerashaivism.

This vachana 51 itself, as given on pages 326 through 331 in volume IV of the referenced Shunya Sampadane (1) says that it gives the fifty-two features, but the vachana only lists thirty-six qualities.

It is stated in the notes and comments section on page 405 in volume IV of the referenced Shunya Sampadane (1) that the portion of the vachana containing the other sixteen characteristics coming at the beginning, is left out in this vachana. The editors also state there that the complete vachana that enumerates all the fifty-two features in it is the vachana number 46 on pages 95 and 96 in the reference - *Uḍutaḍiya Mahādēviyakkanavara Sāhitya.* Edited by Professor B. C. Jawali and Sri Mallabadi Virabhadrappa. Published by Pampasahitya Prakashana, Davangere, 1963. That reference could not be procured for further evaluation.

Mahadeviyakka also praises other Sharanas; they all praise her in response. This back and forth praising goes on in the vachanas of Sharanas.

Association with Sharanas at Kalyana

Mahadeviyakka spends some time at the Academy of Sharanas (Anubhava Mantapa) in Kalyana. It is not clear how long she stayed there. She depicts her experience there in her vachanas. It seems that her fellowship enhanced her spirituality and made her better understand the Sharana way of life.

In one of her vachanas, Mahadeviyakka remarks that by association with the Sharanas, she has acquired the constant joy of Sharana's Truth, and that she has been saved. She implies that this would not have been possible without this companionship with the Sharanas. Vachana 65 on pages 343 and 344 in volume IV of Shunya Sampadane (1) is as follows:

Except through contact,
Fire cannot be kindled;
Except through contact, seed cannot sprout;
Except through contact, body is not born;
Except through contact,
No happiness can come to be.
O Chenna-Mallikarjuna Deva,
Because of Thy Sharanas'
Mystic companionship, I was made
Supremely happy and was saved,
O Prabhu!

In the following vachana, Mahadeviyakka expresses how her spirituality has been enhanced by this association with the Sharanas. Vachana 66 on pages 344 and 345 in volume IV of Shunya Sampadane (1) is something like this:

O Lord, by fellowship with those
Who have experienced Thee,
My body has been purified.
O Lord, because those ones
Who have experienced Thee
Have rubbed and cut and ground me fine
To make me fit for Thee,
My mind has been purified.
Because all my enjoyments of all things
Have been dedicated first to Thy Sharanas,
My soul has been purified.
Because my senses have received
Thy Sharanas' grace,
My entire body has been purified.
O Chenna-Mallikarjunayya,
Because Thy Sharanas made me such,
I am an ornament to Thy Sharanas,
O Prabhu!

In this next vachana, Mahadeviyakka remarks that she attained fulfilment through Basavanna, Chennabasavanna, Allama Prabhudeva, Siddharamayya, Maḍivāḷa Māchayya, and all the innumerable Sharanas.

After spending such time in association with the Sharanas, Mahadeviyakka seems fit to achieve consubstantial union with the Linga.

Enquiring about the Unitive State

When Mahadeviyakka feels that she is ready to proceed to achieve oneness with the Absolute, she wonders when and how this will happen.

In the following vachana, Mahadeviyakka exclaims to Prabhudeva, when the disembodied state will occur.

The Kannada term *'kaḍaḷi'* comes four times in this vachana. This word has been used with different meanings. 'Kadaḷi' is said to mean 'plantain-grove' which may imply that it is a difficult task to perform. Kadaḷi also means sphere of activity, field of expertise, problematic field, range of influence, and such.

Vachana 68 on pages 347 and 348 in volume IV of Shunya Sampadane (1) is as follows:

All the deeds are my sphere of activity;
Field of expertise of the body is yours;
Basavanna's sphere is pious acts, and
Chennabasavanna's is the will.
Our purpose for which we came
Is now accomplished.
O Chenna-Mallikarjuna
O tell me of my body's end.

Allama Prabhudeva responds with one of his difficult to understand vachanas. Vachana 69 on page 348 in volume IV of Shunya Sampadane (1) is as follows:

So long as there is body, one must learn
From association with the Sharanas.
So long as there is soul, one must go
By way of Consciousness.
Until there is Consciousness, your needs
Must have the symbol Guheshvara!

Mahadeviyakka asks Allama Prabhudeva where her unitive state would be – the place, time, and circumstance for her consubstantial union with the Linga.

Prabhudeva complies and gives instruction to Mahadeviyakka about her ultimate union with the Absolute. Vachana 71 on pages 349 and 350 in volume IV of Shunya Sampadane (1) is as follows:

Shedding the duality of You and Me,
And climbing the great mountain of Trikūṭa,
Where your-self becomes the Self, you look,
There, an empty stretch is what you see.
There in the Trikūṭa mountain is a
Plantain-grove (kadaḷi) hidden from view.
If you can enter the ambit of that
Plantain-grove, and look, there is the
Radiance of a flaming light, you hear.
Thither you go, Mother!
In Guheshvara-Linga, the highest peak
Becomes your own, you see!

This is a difficult to understand vachana. Although the vachana does not mention Shrishaila, it is said that the direction is to the Shrishaila Mountain area. The plantain-grove, Kadaḷi, is said to be there on the Shrishaila Mountain. If one can enter the ambit of the plantain-grove, one will see the radiance of a flaming light. 'Go there, the highest peak becomes your own!'

The editors of volume IV of this referenced Shunya Sampadane (1), explain this vachana in the notes and comments section on pages 405 and 406. It is something like this:

First of all she should come after dis-engaging herself from 'I'-ness and 'Thou'-ness, so that there is no sign of duality. Then she has to climb the great mountain of Trikūṭa - this apparently signifies where the self becomes the Self. Here, it is said that one can see the mystery of the numberless universe. Standing on the edge of this great mystery, if one can see the eye of Knowledge that is wide open, one comes to the experience of the Infinite Light and the Absolute Void completely rid of all form.

Those days in the twelfth century, the forested Shrishaila Mountain area was a dreadful and a dangerous place. It is said that it was practically impossible to tread in the forested area. It is not clear how many others, if any, accompanied Mahadeviyakka, primarily to help her accomplish her task. It seems that some Sharanas did accompany her to Shrishaila.

<u>Leaving the city of Kalyana</u>

A time comes when Mahadeviyakka realizes that her stay at Kalyana and association with the great Sharanas has prepared her fully for the attainment of the Absolute. It is not clear how long she stayed at Kalyana. Anyway, she bids farewell to the great Sharanas, and leaves the city of Kalyana.

Mahadeviyakka in her farewell vachana says that she is happy being incorporated with her own lord, and pledges that she will never yield to another and that she will not crave for any pleasures. Vachana 75 on pages 354 and 355 in volume IV of Shunya Sampadane (1) is as follows:

Listen good sirs, I am happy being
Incorporate with mine own lord, who is
Unbounded, disembodied, beyond speech.
My pledge will never fail,
Not to another will I yield myself.
No other pleasures shall I crave again.
Reducing the six to three, the three to two,
The two to one, I live my friends!
Now farewell to the Sharanas,
Basavanna foremost among them!
Through Prabhudeva I attained fulfilment:
Forget not, pray, I am your little child.
Bless me, so I may be made one with
Chenna-Mallikarjuna!

In the above vachana it is not clear what she means by saying that she has reduced six down to one. It seems that she has gone through the six sthalas of Shatsthala and reduced it to one the non-sthala that she had said in one of her previous vachanas.

Mahadeviyakka continues her farewell address in the next vachana, addressing mainly the innumerable Sharanas who had assembled there to send her off. She points out how they nurtured her spiritually, and confirmed her spiritual marriage to Chenna-Mallikarjuna, the Absolute Divine. Vachana 76 on pages 355 through 357 in volume IV of Shunya Sampadane (1) is as follows:

Within the holy Guru's palm I had my birth;
I grew up in the grace of
The innumerable ones;
Behold, they fed me on the milk of love,
On wisdom's ghee (clarified butter),
And sugar of the ultimate Truth!
On these three kinds of nectar
They nurtured me to surfeiting.
My marriage you performed;
Gave me to a worthy groom;
And you the innumerable ones,
Came out in crowds to send me to
My husband's house.
I behave in that house so as to
Please Basavanna;
With hands knit to Chenna-Mallikārjuna's,
I bring flowers to your heads,
But listen pray, never a straw;
Let all your feet do me
The grace of going back.

Hail, O hail! I bow to you!

Then as she was walking out of the city of Kalyana, Mahadeviyakka expresses the sadness of her parting from the innumerable Sharanas. Vachana 77 on page 357 in volume IV of Shunya Sampadane (1) is as follows:

Lord, what comparison can be found for
The happiness of being joined
To your great ones!
Lord, having been with them,
Death is far better than parting from them!
O Chenna-Mallikarjuna, I cannot bear
Parting from the great and glorious ones
Who know the Truth of Thee!

Leaving the city of Kalyana, Mahadeviyakka travels towards the holy place of Shrishaila.

Treading the Forest and the Shrishaila Mountain

Guided by Prabhudeva's direction, Mahadeviyakka makes her way through the forest to Mount Shrishaila.

It is said that the vachanas sung by Akka Mahadevi on the way to Shrishaila, and at Shrishaila itself, apart from being of exquisite lyrical beauty, are gems of mystic utterance (1).

Those days in the twelfth century, the forested Shrishaila Mountain area was a dreadful and a dangerous place. It is said that it was practically impossible to tread in the forested area.

In the following vachana, Mahadeviyakka indicates that, as she entered the forest, for her body's sake she begged the trees for food, and that she will not beg again. Vachana 79 on page 359 in volume IV of Shunya Sampadane (1) is as follows:

Because of body's pangs
I went into the forest;
For body's sake I begged
From tree to tree, not missing one;
And for their Ling's sake they gave me food.
Begging, I turned into a world-ling (bhavi);
They, giving, became the devotees!
O Chenna-Mallikarjunayya,
Thy curse upon me if I beg again!

Mahadeviyakka brings up a point that Sharanas do not beg for ordinary alms including food. She implies that begging makes one to be a bhavi. Bhavi is a world-ling or a miscreant, the one who is subject to the cycle of births and deaths. Bhavi does not believe in the Sharana way of life.

Having arrived at the Shrishaila Mountain, in the forest there, Mahadeviyakka continues to seek her spiritual husband the Absolute Divine Chenna-Mallikarjuna. Vachana 80 on page 360 in volume IV of Shunya Sampadane (1) is as follows:

O swarm of bees, O mango tree,
O cuckoo and the light of moon,
One thing I ask of all of you:
If you catch sight of my lord
Chenna-Mallikarjuna,
Call out and let me see!

Mahadeviyakka continues seeking her beloved spiritual husband. Vachana 81 on pages 360 and 361 in volume IV of Shunya Sampadane (1) is as follows:

O parrots, prattling your shrill patter,
You have not seen Him?
O cuckoos, lifting up your voices,
You have not seen Him?
O bees, that dart and play around,
You have not seen Him?
O swans that frolic on the lakes,
You have not seen Him?
O huntsmen, sporting over hills and dales,

You have not seen Him; or have you?
Tell me, O tell me, where my
Chenna-Mallikarjuna is!

Continuing, Mahadeviyakka directly addresses the Absolute Divine. Vachana 82 on page 361 in volume IV of Shunya Sampadane (1) is as follows:

The entire forest art Thou!
The sacred trees within the forest art Thou!
The birds and bees that sport
Among the trees art Thou!
O Chenna-Mallikarjuna,
When Thou pervades everything,
Why dost not show Thyself to me?

In the above vachana, Mahadeviyakka brings out the point that the Absolute Divinity pervades everything.

Having arrived at Shrishaila Mountain, Mahadeviyakka climbs the mountain and continues to seek the Divine. It is said that her journey was fraught with difficulties and dangers. But Mahadeviyakka faced everything as the face of the Divine.

She sets up camp there at Shrishaila Mountain, and spends some time there. It is not clear how long she was there in the mountain. But it is said that she was there until she was about twenty-five years of age.

Here in the Shrishaila Mountain, Mahadeviyakka's yearning for union with the Divine Chenna-Mallikarjuna grows intense.

In the following vachana, Mahadeviyakka implies that although she had desires in the past, she has come there and has climbed the holy mountain without any desires. Vachana 84 on pages 362 and 363 in volume IV of Shunya Sampadane (1) is as follows:

While action lasts, that is one desire;
While words of true-devotees persist,
That is one more desire.
If I, climbing the holy mountain,
Unite with Thee, O Lord,
Will that be the end of all desires?
Trusting to Thee I came without desire,
And now I am undone,
O Chenna-Mallikarjuna!

In the next vachana, Mahadeviyakka continues her pleading of the Absolute Divine. Vachana 85 on pages 363 and 364 in volume IV of Shunya Sampadane (1) is as follows:

Shall I say Bayalu (Void/space) is Linga?
Walk and cleave through it, it is gone!
Shall I say mountain is Linga?
Climb and stand on it, it is gone!
Shall I say trees and shrubs are Linga?
You cut them, it is gone!
I did not heed the words of
Sangana Basavanna saying that the feet of

Linga and Jangama themselves are the goal,
Thus I am lost, O Chenna-Mallikarjuna!

Mahadeviyakka displays her yearning for union with the Divine Chenna-Mallikarjuna. Pleading with intense true-devotion, Mahadeviyakka continues contemplation in order to attain the unitive state. Vachana 86 on page 364 in volume IV of Shunya Sampadane (1) is as follows:

Quickly, O quickly, show Thyself,
And Thou unite Thyself with me;
Do not dismiss me, Lord!
I am a maid attached to Thee;
Do not reject me, Lord!
O Chenna-Mallikarjunayya,
Trusting in Thee, I followed Thee;
Quickly, O quickly, take me, Lord,
Into Thy arms!

Then, Mahadeviyakka finds the plantain-grove (kadaḷi).

Kadaḷi: The Plantain-grove

Allama Prabhudeva had given the direction to the Shrishaila Mountain, and to the plantain-grove (kadaḷi). Accordingly, Mahadeviyakka was able to find the plantain-grove.

In her vachana, Mahadeviyakka describes her arrival there at the plantain-grove. Vachana 87 on page 365 in volume IV of Shunya Sampadane (1) is as follows:

The entire forest is a wishing-tree;
The life-restoring are all these shrubs;
Every stone is alchemic-stone
Every spot is a holy place;
All water is un-ageing nectar;
Every beast is a man-like beast,
And the stone you tumble on
Is the wishing-stone.
On arrival, as I looked around the mountain
Loved of Chenna-Mallikarjunayya,
I saw the Plantain-grove!

Allama Prabhudeva had indicated to Mahadeviyakka of what to expect there when she would enter the plantain-grove: If one can enter the ambit of the plantain-grove, one will see the radiance of a flaming light. 'Go there, the highest peak becomes your own!'

Now that Mahadeviyakka enters the plantain-grove, this is what is said to occur: The Light of the Divine Consciousness within her, presents itself in front of her in the form of a Jangama.

In her vachana, Mahadeviyakka describes this Jangama as splendid with glowing ruddy hair, with bright teeth, shining eyes, smiling face, and a ruby crown. Vachana 88 on pages 366 and 367 in volume IV of Shunya Sampadane (1) is as follows:

Seeing the radiant form
That lights the fourteen worlds
With the splendor of His eyes,
His ruddy shining hair,
His white teeth, His smiling countenance,
And His comely ruby crown,
The hunger of my eyes is now appeased!
I have seen the great one who lords over
Lords and lords as if they were his wives!
Seeing the majesty of Chenna-Mallikarjuna,
The Great Guru who, in union with the
Primordial power, speaks,
I have been saved!

It is said in the prose section of the referenced Shunya Sampadane (1), that Mahadeviyakka, seeing the Jangama form, bowed to it, spoke its praise, and humbly said:

'O the Divine, in dread of the assault of all my senses, I surrendered to Thy Sharanas. After obtaining their grace, I came here and beheld Thy holy face. Now make me one with Thee O Chenna-Mallikarjuna!'

And it is also said that the Jangama who was the Consciousness, saying 'Come, my daughter who have come here after shedding the bonds of birth', embraced her, and so Mahadeviyakka attained her unitive state. (1).

Mahadeviyakka's vachana which is said to tell all the above mentioned passage is given here. It is to be pointed out that the term 'kadaḷi' comes six times in this vachana. The vachana seems to describe what kadaḷi means. The kadaḷi has been translated as 'plantain-grove'. But, here, in the vachana given below the term 'kadaḷi' has been retained in order to make a better sense of it. Vachana 89 on page 368 in volume IV of Shunya Sampadane (1) is as follows:

What is called kadaḷi is the body;
What is called kadaḷi is the mind;
What is called kadaḷi is the infirmity of sense,
What is kadaḷi is the dread forest of life.

This kadaḷi have I subdued,
And here have I come safe and sound,
To see Him who destroys the wheel of births,
Within this kadaḷi.

When He drew me into His arms,
Compassionately, as though I was his child
Come back, untainted of the world,
I hid myself within the lotus of the heart
Of Chenna-Mallikarjuna!

The Divine Chenna-Mallikarjuna is The Light of the Divine Consciousness within her. It is her own Self.

With Mahadeviyakka saying she hid herself within the lotus of the heart of her spiritual husband Chenna-Mallikarjuna, she attained her unitive state where everything is only one.

The Unitive State

Mahadeviyakka who attained the unitive state, describes this unitive state as 'Silence'. She is said to have been lost in silence. Vachana 90 on page 369 in volume IV of Shunya Sampadane (1) is something like this:

I cannot say it is Linga.
I cannot say it is oneness with Linga.
I cannot say it is union.
I cannot say it is harmony.
I cannot say it has occurred.
I cannot say it has not occurred.
I cannot say it is Thou.
I cannot say it is I.
Once I have become
One with the Absolute Linga,
In Chenna-Mallikarjuna-Linga
I can say nothing at all!

This unitive state has also been described in the referenced Shunya Sampadane (1) as - like hailstone melting in water, like a packet of salt dissolving in water, like milk mixing with milk, like vanishing, and such.

It is said that the vachanas sung by Akka Mahadevi on the way to Shrishaila, and at Shrishaila itself, apart from being of exquisite lyrical beauty, are gems of mystic utterance.

As has been indicated before, there are a total of 354 vachanas of Akka Mahadevi. All these vachanas can be accessed and researched in the referenced Ganaka Vachana Samputa (3). Most of these vachanas have also been translated to English in that reference (3).

When one reviews all the vachanas of Mahadeviyakka in order to better understand her concept of the Sharana Philosophy and Practice, it becomes obvious that Mahadeviyakka's vachanas also conform to what the vachanas of other Sharanas stand for. This may be because Mahadeviyakka had stayed for some time with the Sharanas at the Academy of the Sharanas, the assembly hall called Anubhava Mantapa. (29).

Some of the information on the philosophical aspects in Mahadeviyakka's vachanas is given in the referenced book (29).

There are 92 vachanas in this sixteenth chapter. The subtotal so far comes to 1,095 vachanas.

The fifth volume starts with the seventeenth chapter.

Chapter 17

SAMPĀDANE OF PRABHUDĒVA'S TOUR AND RETURN

When the Sharanas were extolling Mahadeviyakka's unitive state, Prabhudeva says 'I will see you again', and bids goodbye to the Sharanas.

At that juncture, Siddharamayya also takes leave of them. He requests Prabhudeva to tell him how he should be united unto the Absolute – whether he should dwell within the higher abode (Sahasrāra/Brahmarandhra) situated above the three-levels, or dwell in the central hall (heart).

In response, Prabhudeva explains to Siddharamayya the Sharana's spiritual life:

Sharana's birth is a spiritual birth at the hands of a spiritual Guru. The entire being of Sharana, divested of human nature, merges in the Light of Consciousness. This may occur in three ways – after losing the body at a natural death; laying aside the body voluntarily; or **attaining to the Absolute along with the body where the corporeal existence is transformed into ethereal existence.** True ecstasy is when, after shedding the stark illusion, one attains the ecstasy of body, sense and soul. **That is the enlightened ecstasy in the Absolute.**

Readers, please note that the Veerashaiva concept is simple – it is not the union in the higher abode situated above the three levels, or in the middle heart lotus; it is all one and only one; **the entire being, divested of human nature, merges in the Light of Consciousness**.

It is said in the prose section of Shunya Sampadane that Prabhudeva moved about among different places. Prabhudeva's course of wanderings is very briefly described here:

Jangama Prabhudeva walked all over India to sanctify the land and return to Kalyana. He visited Ponnāṁbalanātha, and had conversations on mystic life with those he found there who then won serenity through the dawning of the knowledge within them. He then wandered along the coast of the eastern sea going south to Rāmeshvaram. There he held a happy conference with Rāmanātha and received worship. From there he beheld the southern sea and then the western sea. He visited Mahābaleshvara. From there he turned towards north and visited Somanātha in Saurashtra. There he released the birth-bonds of all those who saw and heard him. Departing from there, he visited several holy places and gave them wondrous boons. Then he visited sixty-eight bathing places; having received worship from those bathing there, gave them pure Ganga (Ganges River) water which is the essence of the Supreme Bliss. From there he wandered from one place to another sanctifying them. Then he arrived at Shrīkēdāra, and from there resisting very intense cold and snow, made his sojourn among mountains and caves in the region of the south of the Himalayas which constituted part of Kashmir. After finding a cave, vast enough and suitable enough for him, he stayed there for a while.

There he sat in a lotus position; focused his mind, breath, reason, knowledge and thought on one point, and remained in that will-less condition in a state of consubstantial union until he realized *Nisshunya* –Void of Voids; and got transfixed in the ultimate trance.

It is said that, after attaining this trance, the radiant Prabhudeva, shining in all splendor, rose and went in the direction of the city of Kalyana.

Meanwhile, at Kalyana, Basavanna Knowing that Prabhudeva would return to Kalyana, erected the Throne of the Absolute *(Shunya-siṁhāsana)* in the Anubhava Mantapa with the expectation of Prabhudeva's arrival.

Haḍapada Appaṇṇa, an assistant to Basavanna, describes the Throne of the Absolute in his vachanas. It is said that the structure and the materials used for the throne as described in the vachanas are symbolic of the process through which Basavanna attained to the realization of the Absolute.

After erecting the Throne of the Absolute and putting up the flags and festoons, Basavanna eagerly awaits Prabhudeva's arrival. In one of his vachanas, Basavanna indicates that twelve years' time has passed since Prabhudeva had said 'I will see you again', and had bid goodbye to the Sharanas. Thus, Prabhudeva is returning to Kalyana after twelve years' time.

Basavanna sees Prabhudeva's arrival and describes Prabhudeva's appearance to Chennabasavanna. It is a hideous picture of Prabhudeva. Basavanna adds that despite his appearance, Prabhudeva's nature is perfectly free from taint.

Basavanna continues 'Look, there is no shadow where he stands, no footprint where he walks, nowhere upon earth is seen such a strange motion, certainly he is an inscrutable Jangama'.

Prabhudeva comes and stands in front of the gate of Basavanna's place.

There are 59 vachanas in this seventeenth chapter. The subtotal comes to 1,154 vachanas.

Chapter 18

SAMPĀDANE OF PRABHUDĒVA'S ASCENSION ON THE THRONE OF THE ABSOLUTE

This eighteenth chapter begins with Prabhudeva entering Basavanna's place. In the prose section of the chapter, there is an elaborate description of the decorations of the inside of Basavanna's place; the decorations are said to be symbolic representations of the spiritual activities and such. The vachanas of the Sharanas describe Prabhudeva's majesty transcending all boundaries of form, time and space. Then Basavanna worships Prabhudeva's feet, and says that he has come to know Prabhudeva as his Pranalinga Itself, and that he has found the treasure that must not be lost.

As Basavanna was worshipping Prabhudeva with sincere devotion, and also singing and dancing with joy, numerous Jangamas who were sitting at dinner there got up in anger and went away.

Prabhudeva responds by saying – 'the world of gods is what is within, the mortal world is what is without, since we are away from those two worlds, let them be there; they are all but a horde of flesh assembled for the sake of food; they cannot know Guheshvara's (the Absolute's) majesty'.

Chennabasavanna also ridicules those Jangamas: Those who may have a shaven head and wear the garb, and also indulge in worldly pleasures, are not true Jangamas.

Basavanna repents at the departure of the Jangamas: 'If Jangama is angry, my breath departs; how can I live should a Jangama rage?'

Prabhudeva consoles him: 'There is no need to worry or fear; the glory of the heart does not depart you fool, there is no place for parting; one can serve a Jangama only when all symbol – be it on the palm, the body, mind or life – is abolished, and one stands as free and pure and perfect as is the Jangama-Linga itself'.

Prabhudeva then asks Basavanna: I have come to beg for alms of piety; Guheshvara is hungry; give me the alms of piety. This Prabhudeva's vachana exemplifies the cardinal feature of the Jangama - **Jangama does not beg for ordinary alms of food and such; the Jangama asks for complete surrender to the Supreme.** Basavanna understands and responds appropriately: For Linga's sake I serve you spiritual food; without desire, without fancy, without thought, and without delusion I serve unto your plate; accept it with good grace.

Prabhudeva: There is no ending to your flow of words! Guheshvara is hungry, serve the food!

Basavanna says: I do not know the niceties of saying it is pure or saying it is good; and I do not yet know what offering is; so, if I serve it as it is, you accept it as it comes.

Prabhudeva says enough of your modesty; only you on earth know how to appease Guheshvara-Linga's hunger.

Then, upon Basavanna saying 'when Prabhudeva worships I attend to him', Prabhudeva begins his Linga-worship. It is the worship of the Infinite Linga by the Infinite Jangama. There is no longer an inner and an outer; it is the Infinite singing its own glory!

There are 59 vachanas in this eighteenth chapter. The subtotal so far is 1,213 vachanas.

Chapter 19

PRABHUDĒVA'S FEAST

Prabhudeva seated on the Throne of the Absolute (Shūnya Siṁhāsana), completes his worship. Wives of the Sharanas sing praise to Prabhudeva, and all the Sharanas amidst the clangor of the five great instruments are delighted. Basavanna thinking that Prabhudeva might eat, brings a plate, sets it down and says:

'For the embodied Linga, the body is the plate; for the Linga in the soul, the mind is the plate; for the Linga in the consciousness, the will-less-ness is the plate; and when Prabhudeva is to eat, it is the plate of piety'.

Prabhudeva at that juncture, states something like this: 'When food was made ready and various courses came in various ways, before they were seen, the form itself became an offering; before they were touched, the touch itself became an offering; before they were tasted, the relish itself became an offering; O Linga, do eat Basavanna's gift! What is offered in the body is not an offering; what is offered in the soul is not an offering; nor is what is offered in the will and consciousness; **attentive service without the thought of giving, eating without forgetfulness, that is an offering; that is not touched at all'**.

It is said that as Basavanna was serving without pause, and Prabhudeva was gobbling it all up in no time. Prabhudeva seemed to have many faces on all sides, and seemed to eat through mouths cropping up all around. The food seemed to vanish even before it was served, and Basavanna seemed helpless despite the help from other Sharanas.

Basavanna and the other Sharanas were bewildered, and were wondering what would be the art of satisfying Prabhudeva.

It is said that Chennabasavanna then speaks of the one and the same identity between the feeder and the fed, which is a fundamental concept of the Oneness Philosophy. When Chennabasavanna says to Basavanna 'you should be the main dish, the side dish I; it is the only way to feed Prabhudeva', he supposedly means - **it is only the Infinite love that can feed an Infinite Divine.**

Then Basavanna says something like this: 'When wealth is spent out, I offer my body; when my body is spent out, I offer my mind; when mind is spent out, I offer my will; when will is spent out, I offer will-less-ness. I offer thee food never touched by place; I dedicate all to Thee and be purified'.

Chennabasavanna then says something like this: 'What is offered to you is what you have given; Guru is food, and disciple is side dish; this is an offering for Linga, but mind is the offering to the Absolute; and when the mind is incorporated into the Absolute, who is the devotee to serve and who is the God to eat? What else to serve O Prabhudeva, Basavanna is the main dish, the side dish I; eat then with good cheer'.

The Jangama feeds on the Bhakta, and is completely satisfied; and the Bhakta is fulfilled in offering his self to the Jangama.

Prabhudeva, satisfied, says something like this in his vachana – 36 on page 178 in volume V of Shunya Sampadane (1) is as follows:

As piety was the course,
Truth the trimmings, and
Reality the sweet,
There is none else but
Sangana Basavanna
To know the way to serve
Guheshvara-Linga.

It is said that the individual Spirit is one though it dwells in different bodies. In the essential unity of Bhakta and Jangama, the Jangama is the vital principle breathing through the Bhakta.

They all praise one another. Then Basavanna requests Prabhudeva how to ease the anger of the Jangamas who had walked out of dinner earlier.

Prabhudeva says something like this:

'The Divine is above good and evil; it transcends all duality; and it is not apart from the Jangama Community. Mere symbol, divested for what it stands for, has no meaning; it is a sculptor's creation; the true Linga cannot be made. The Jangamas' garments mean nothing if they have not realized the meaning of life; those whose actions are inspired by egoism are doomed to destruction. Discipline does not bind to Sharana who knows, and Sharana does not need Linga when he has discipline. A Sharana has to go beyond Linga and its worship, and beyond knowledge and discipline'.

Basavanna says that he considers both form representing the Jangamas and the formless Prabhudeva are equally important, and that there is no point in demonizing one and glorifying the other.

Prabhudeva responds:

'I am both form and formlessness. Will is the life breath of form whereas the supreme Knowledge is the vital essence of the formlessness. Both these are essential qualities; without either one, there is no meaning'.

Then Prabhudeva praises Basavanna for removing his taint of anger and making him to attain the Absolute. And then tells him to go where the angry Jangamas are, calm them by asking for forgiveness, and bring them back.

Basavanna does what Prabhudeva told him to do. Then, Chennabasavanna observes that when Prabhudeva is content, all beings, let alone those Jangamas, are content.

Then there is this praising among the Sharanas. There are about 77 consecutive vachanas of praising in this part of the chapter. Prabhudeva and Basavanna praise each other, and after that they all praise one another.

There are 159 vachanas in this nineteenth chapter, with the subtotal coming to 1,372 vachanas.

Chapter 20

PROPHECY OF THE SHARAṆAS' END

When all the Sharaṇas were praising Prabhudeva and also one another, Prabhudeva says that there is no use in indulging in mere praise; it is not possible to reach the Silent Brahman by the string of words of praise; the mission for which all of them came has been fulfilled; they have to understand for themselves that they have to attain the Reality in quietude.

This splendid vachana of Prabhudeva – vachana 1 on pages 299 and 300 in volume V of Shunya Sampadane (1) – is as follows:

Unless you know that which you are,
Unless you meditate your origin,
And unless you see your soul in timelessness,
What is the use of praise?
You simpletons, can you attain by praise
The Absolute that is called
'The silent Brahman'?

From immemorial time, Basavanna with
Seven-hundred-seventy immortal saints,
Came down upon this earth with a purpose.
And the mission wherefore he came
Is now fulfilled.
Listen ye assembled ancient saints,
Henceforth, you should attain Reality,

You, one and all,
By understanding for yourselves,
Henceforth, our Guheshvara-Linga knows
No motion of a form!

And then, Prabhudeva commands them: *'Ancient saints, Basavanna and Chennabasavanna among you, attain Reality and rest in peace'.*

Then Basavanna asks Prabhudeva to tell him how his (Basavanna's) consubstantial union between Anga and Linga would take place.

Prabhudeva says something like this:

- The less you speak about Reality, the deeper you live in the Linga-effulgence, and the faster you advance towards the ultimate Reality Shunya.
- When there is complete transformation of oneself into the Divine-self, there is no more to be taught and no more to be learnt.
- No amount of reasoning, feeling or action will lend one to such experience.
- As long as there is the experience of the utmost tranquility filled with Divine Grace, all talk is vain.

Then Prabhudeva says that Basavanna is not only a divine being, but also the very syllables of his name – ba, sa, va – are impregnated with divinity. The state of Guru, Linga, Jangama and Prasada has not only merged within the symbol on his palm, but also have all been incorporated in himself.

Then Prabhudeva says: Those who have gone to Kailāsa (Shiva's abode) have been imprisoned; those who have reached different levels of salvation move up and down; but Basavanna, by taking the grace of Jangama has himself become Linga. The vachana 21 on page 319 in volume V of Shunya Sampadane (1) is something like this:

The travelers to Kailāsa (Shiva's abode)
Have been made captive;
All who have merged
Without becoming one in Liṅga
Have earned but bonds;
And those who have reached
Sālōkya, Sāmīpya, Sārūpya, and Sāyujya,
All move up and down.
O Guheshvara,
Sangana Basavanna, Thy Sharaṇa,
By taking the grace of Jangama,
Has, in himself, been deified!

The first three items in the above vachana apply to the dvaitas – followers of the duality who believe that the individual self is different from God. Sālōkya refers to those going to the place of God after death, Sāmīpya applies to those who stay in proximity to God, Sārūpya to those taking the form of the God, and Sāyujya to those who merge in the God but do not become God itself. But Basavanna taking the grace of Jangama has become God.

Then Prabhudeva describes Shunya in his songs:

- This highest state is achieved when one's whole being, including love and devotion, knowledge and yoga, worship and action, are all dissolved into the Absolute and made one with the Absolute.
- In the Absolute state there is no individual consciousness or any other consciousness; there is no meditation; the trinity of knower, knowledge and known has also ceased; there is no in or out; there is no remembrance or forgetfulness; the overpowering discriminative consciousness is not there; when fire and camphor join and both burn out, there is no ash left, similarly, when the root of consciousness is burnt, there is no ash of knowledge left.
- Losing all seeking in the ultimate Truth, all sense and reason having ceased, the effulgent Spirit gets extinguished in itself; that is Non-Void (it also means the Absolute).
- With the sense of 'mine' destroyed, with the sense of 'I' reduced to naught, the Glory beyond compare has become the seat of pure Reality.
- Standing in oneself as radiance of the light of consciousness, and the sense which says 'I am' becoming naught, the tranquil dwelling in oneself oblivious of oneself, one who transcends the consciousness is the incomparable, the tranquil and impenetrable.
- Sound turned to silence, silence turned to un-struck sound, the very sense of sound and

silence vanish; unconscious of what is or what is gone, one is silent deep.

In addition to Prabhudeva, Basavanna, and Chennabasavanna, seven other Sharanas, namely Maḍivāḷayya, Bahurupa Choudayya, Haḍapada Appaṇṇa, Soḍḍaḷa Bācharasa, Akka-Nāgāyi, Mōḷige Mārayya, and Dohara Kakkayya, give an account of their progress in their spiritual path to attain their goal.

Prabhudeva makes a prophecy about himself; it is as follows:

- Beyond the sharpest point of mind, the awareness having stayed birth and death, the dawn of the glowing knowledge transcending myriad suns, what shall I say of the Glory of the Absolute that absorbs the dawn of self-experience?
- I have been beyond self-consciousness in the Truth; there is nothing to be seen; there is nothing to be heard; how shall I describe one which is made of the splendor that proceeds from the vast Immaculate?
- Seeing the Glory, my mind seized it; as it gazed and gazed, the mind was turned into the Absolute; it dissolved in it until it became one with it; how shall I explain the sound transforming into Silence?
- Cannot taste the sweetness of ecstasy of the wondrous Void; cannot find the word to say 'I cannot see'; having known the knowledge that can do without the sign, I blush to use the hollow word that says 'I merged'.

- Comparison, powerless to compare, declared it was beyond compare; awareness, unaware that it was screened from knowledge, declared that it was higher than the highest; Meditation not knowing to meditate, was lost in meditation itself as it transcended all efforts of meditation; there is no other knowledge to knower, knowledge and the known; 'That Thou art' and other great sayings the Veda regards as knowledge are gone; all who expound Brahman – the dualists and the non-dualists – as Being, Consciousness and Bliss, are routed and destroyed. It comes and does not come; it gets and does not get; it is one, the Absolute Tranquility.
- Being one with the body which the Guru transformed, Guru is nothing now; being one with the soul which Linga had transformed, Linga is nothing now; being one with the mind which Jangama had transformed, Jangama is nothing now; being one with the teacher who had taught the triple piety, both teacher and I have been saved.
- 'I' is a limitation; 'Thou' is a limitation; the 'Self' is limitation; the 'Supreme' is limitation; limitation itself is limitation; **the Absolute alone is limitless.**

There are 92 vachanas in this twentieth chapter; the subtotal so far is 1,464 vachanas.

Chapter 21

GŌRAKSHA'S SAMPADANE, AND ALL SAINTS' AIKYA

Prabhudeva relates to all the Saints the circumstances of their final end. He relates this in his vachana:

'Our time has lapsed; parting is all that is left. True Sharanas can no longer live in this age. Basavanna, you go to Sangama Deva at Kappaḍi. Chennabasavanna you go to Ulavi (a place in Karnataka) and attain Reality there. Maḍivāḷayya, you unite yourself with the Great Light. Soḍḍaḷa Bācharasa and all the Saints, in a space-less trance attain the Truth. Those who can proceed to Kailāsa with their body, go penetrate your way into Linga. This sacred counsel is that you arrive with your body. For me the final place must be to enter the plantain grove and there unite with the Absolute. For all of you this is Guheshvara-Linga's behest'.

Encounter with Gōraksha

Prabhudeva, after bidding farewell to all the Sharanas, leaves the city of Kalyana. As he was going towards the holy Shrishaila Mountain, he meets an accomplished yogi named Gōraksha. This yogi, with his siddhi (Hatha yoga), apparently had made his body as hard as a diamond so that it could even repel a sharp sword. It is said in the prose section of Shunya Sampadane that Prabhudeva tested Gōraksha's adamantine body and saw the result himself.

The subsequent legendary part of the story is not given in Shunya Sampadane. This part of the story is that Prabhudeva asks Gōraksha to use the sword on Prabhudeva's body. When Gōraksha swings the sword, it just goes through Prabhudeva's body without causing any type of injury. Prabhudeva had the so called ethereal body so that no harm can come to it.

Prabhudeva criticizes Gōraksha's accomplishment of physical feat and possession of various yogic tricks. Prabhudeva tells him that this type of yoga, even up to the end, keeps the difference between the performer of the yoga and the object of the yoga; it does not result in the union of the two.

Gōraksha convinced by Prabhudeva of the connection between Anga and Linga, gives up his tricks, and obtains initiation. Prabhudeva then reveals the secret of the space-less trance: When one has come to the complete unitive consciousness, and the consciousness has dissolved into the Absolute, there are no more words like 'I am not', 'who am I', 'I am Parabrahman', and so on.

After the above encounter, Prabhudeva proceeds to the plantain grove in the Shrishaila Mountain.

Prabhudēva at Kadaḷi in Shrīshaila

Prabhudeva compares the plantain grove (kadaḷi) to the dreadful personal body, and describes how he conquered it both outside and inside. The concept of kadaḷi is not completely clear. Mahadeviyakka describes kadaḷi in her vachana; it is given in chapter sixteen in this book.

As in chapter sixteen, the kadaḷi has been translated as 'plantain-grove'. In the vachana given below the term 'kadaḷi' has been retained in order to make a better sense of it. Vachana 11 on page 397 in volume V of Shunya Sampadane (1) is something like this:

Entering the kadaḷi of the body, as I
Came wandering through different rooms
Called the senses in the cave of life,
The day dawned in the triple room
Of the Meru shrine,
Guheshvara-Linga assumed a form!

Prabhudeva, then, goes into the plantain-grove (kadaḷi) and becomes one with the Absolute. The following vachana of Prabhudeva – vachana 12 on pages 398 through 400 in volume V of Shunya Sampadane (1) – is Prabhudeva's last vachana in Shunya Sampadane. It is as follows:

I see no one who can conquer the body's vast kadaḷi,
The seven seas of the worldly life encircle it.

In the life's forest the poisonous rain of the five senses pours.

Anger's huge tiger roars and roars;

The elephants of eight prides are stamping about;

The counter-shafted rain of lust is pouring;

Enormous serpent of jealousy is spitting fire;

That child of sin called greed is chewing and eating;

The triple pain, like rain of fire, will not permit your stepping out;

Mountains of ego have fallen across the path;

You cannot face the fear of ghosts called the five elements;

The ogress Maya devours raw flesh;
The well of passions cannot be used;
Infatuation's creeper tangles your feet
The sharp edged sword of covetousness
Is not to be unsheathed...

Unable to go into this kadaḷi, gods, demons, men have all gone crazy and run off;

Those who have eyes upon their soles,
Those who have eyes all over themselves,
Have lost their heads and tails.

But I have entered that kadaḷi,
Have fought my way, and
Never touched by thorn or bramble,
Have roamed and overcome the kadaḷi,
And crossed it safe;
And dwelling in the ultimate trance of

Guheshvara-Linga, lost in ecstasy,
I am more tranquil than tranquility!

Allama Prabhudeva, in the ultimate trance of Guheshvara-Linga, lost in ecstasy, is now more tranquil than tranquility!

As Prabhudeva attains the ultimate state, Basavanna, Chennabasavanna, and others eulogize Prabhudeva.

Revolution at Kalyana

Then, on the occasion of the inter-caste marriage of the children of Haḷḷayya a cobbler and Madhuvayya a Brahmin, Basavanna was rolling in joy with them. This did not go well with king Bijjala. Basavanna was serving Bijjala as his prime-minister. Bijjala orders that the fathers of bride and bridegroom be tortured and killed. This incident of their killing was the precipitating cause of the hurried departure from Kalyana of Basavanna and the Sharanas.

Basavanna sensing a violent reaction from among his more headlong followers, pacifies them. He then resigns from his position as the Prime-minister to King Bijjala. And upon receiving farewell from innumerable saints, sends them away, and hurriedly leaves Kalyana and goes to Kudala Sangama.

King Bijjala gets killed in the hands of Shiva devotees.

Gūḷūra Siddhavīraṇārya, the composer of the referenced fourth version of Shunya Sampadane (1) makes **a point in dispute.** The dispute is the saying in this Shunya Sampadane that Basavanna himself, directly or indirectly, was responsible for the death of Bijjala.

On page 406 of volume V, it is stated in the prose section that Basavaṇṇa gave orders to Jagadeva to proclaim the truth by slaying Bijjaḷa the ill-wisher of the devotees of Shiva. And then on the same page gives Basavaṇṇa's vachana which states 'Bijjaḷa must die at Jagadeva and Molleya Bommaṇṇa's hand'.

However, first it is to be pointed out that the same Basavaṇṇa's vachana is in the Gaṇaka Vachana Saṁpuṭa reference (3), but there, this vachana 625 does not include that type of statement.

Furthermore, the editors of volume V of the referenced fourth version of Shūnya Saṁpādane (1) in the introduction part on page 378 of volume V, state - 'This is not in perfect conformity with the facts of history as have since come to light', and refer to pages 7 and 8 in volume II of Shūnya Saṁpādane for the explanation. It is stated there in volume II that some writings claim that Basavaṇṇa himself was directly or indirectly responsible for the death of Bijjaḷa, and that even Shūnya Saṁpādane seems to accept this view, but the two prose passages in the fourth version of Shūnya Saṁpādane was a later addition, and that this type of account of what happened is not found in the first two older versions of Shūnya Saṁpādane compiled by Shivagaṇaprasādi Mahādēvayya and by Halageyadēva.

Then the editors say that Siṅgirāja, the author of Siṅgirāja Purāṇa, relates how Basavaṇṇa pacified his followers and averted the danger to Bijjala's life. At the time of assassination of Bijjaḷa, Basavaṇṇa had already left Kalyāṇa. More than all this, there is the entire personality of Basavaṇṇa as revealed by his own vachanas and in those of his contemporaries as well as of his immediate successors, which indicate that Basavaṇṇa was incapable of any type of violent action, let alone a murder.

Last days of Basavanna at Kudala Sangama

Basavanna, after reaching Kappaḍi, sends Haḍapada Appaṇṇa, his assistant, to bring his wife Nīlalōchane to Kappaḍi. But Nīlalōchane does not want to go there, and says 'it does not matter whether I am here or there; through attainment of the Absolute, I enjoy the ultimate bliss; there is no separation between Basavanna and me'. Appaṇṇa comes back and reports to Basavanna. Basavanna accepts his wife's decision.

Basavanna continuing his intense internal worship and meditation remarks that he is ready for the Union (Aikya) and that he does not want any other place in the body of Kudala Sangama Deva (his highest Divinity) but only on the one seat throne in the innermost core of the heart lotus.

It is said that, at that juncture, because Basavanna had gotten Prabhudeva's merciful grace, the Linga of the Higher Consciousness appears in splendor to Basavanna at the center of his innermost mind. Saṅgamēshvara (another name for Kudala Sangama Deva) comes in the form of a Jangama, and embracing Basavanna and so absorbing him in the lotus of his heart, draws Basavanna into Linga.

Basavanna's last vachana in Shunya Sampadane – vachana 48 on pages 426 and 427 in volume V - is as follows:

Between the earth and sky
Was born a mango-tree;
Two boughs it had, three leaves
And thirty-six flowers, and but a single fruit;
Which when filled with juice, nothing I saw;
When the leaves dropped,
The stem loosening, the fruit fell.

Prabhudeva, eating of that fruit,
Vanished into the Absolute.

Because I got Prabhu's merciful grace,
Kudala Sangama Deva saying 'come here',
Placed me within the lotus of His heart.

On page 526 in volume V of Shūnya Saṁpādane (1), the editors give an explanation for this volume. It is given below with minor modification:

- The mango-tree means 'the great tree'; it is the vast tree of 'Liṅga the Divine'.
- The two branches represent 'Aṅga and Liṅga'.
- Each of these (Aṅga and Liṅga) has three parts represented in the vachana as three leaves – gross body, subtle body and causal body, and Ishṭaliṅga, Prāṇaliṅga and Bhāvaliṅga.
- The thirty-six flowers in the vachana represent the thirty-six parts (tattvas) that come in a sequence during creation – a modification of Parashivabrahman. (See 'The Creation' article in this book for more information.)
- The vachana says that there was only one fruit. This fruit, according to the editors is the fruit of *'sarvāĉārasaṁpattu'* which when ripened turned into the ultimate consummation. This completely ripened fruit is said to be worthy of Prabhudēva's eating.
- Further, Prabhudēva, eating that fruit, vanished into the Absolute. Became the Absolute itself.
- Because Basavaṇṇa had gotten Prabhudēva's merciful grace, Kūḍala-Saṅgama-Dēva (the Absolute Divine) embracing Basavaṇṇa and absorbing him, drew Basavaṇṇa into Liṅga the Divine.

It is also said that, at that moment (mentioned above), Sharanas' songs everywhere resounded with acclamation.

All Saints' Aikya

Wife Nīlalōchane mourns. One of her vachanas – vachana 53 on pages 431 and 432 in volume V of Shunya Sampadane (1) – is as follows:

What is there for me after my husband has won the ultimate state?
I have no body, and no life force.
Now that the responsibility to the heart is cancelled, I am but the partaker of the Bliss,
O Saṅgayya!

And subsequently Basavanna's wife Nīlalōchane unites herself in her own Linga. Vachana 57 on page 435 in volume V of Shunya Sampadane (1) is as follows:

O Lord, the Linga on the palm has vanished from my sight;
The Linga on the palm is turned to Linga in my mind...
O Saṅgayya, Basava is gone his way beyond,
And I am merging into you, my Lord!

Basavanna's sister Akkanāgamma laments. One of her vachanas – vachana 62 on pages 439 and 440 in volume V of Shunya Sampadane (1) – is as follows:

Basavanna, when you came down to earth,
Devotion's crop spread everywhere!
Who knows, O brother, how great it is
The harvest of your piety,
On earth, in heaven and in hell?

If you have joined Linga because the mission you were sent for by the moon-holder (Shiva) is complete, devotion too has gone with you!

Right discipline has gone with you!
The innumerable saints are gone with you!
O brother! The Great House of this earth
Is emptied now, Basavanna!
Alas! You have gone leaving me behind.
O incarnation of five alchemies,
Basavanna, you went away as
Pranalinga to
Basavaṇṇapriya Chenna-Saṅgayya,
Sangana Basavanna!

And subsequently Akkanāgamma, Basavanna's elder sister becomes united with Linga.

Chennabasavanna, Akkanāgamma's son, seems to be in utter despair. He makes his remarks at this occasion in vachana 64 on pages 442 and 443 in volume V of Shunya Sampadane (1). It is as follows:

You showed that Linga is Jangama and Jangama is Linga, O true Guru Basavanna, and then you joined the Absolute!

You proved Prasada to be body, and body is Prasada in all my limbs, and then making me what I am, you went ahead Basavanna!

Establishing within the heart that Linga is Prana and Prana is Linga, and making me like you, you vanished out of form, Basavanna, in the great Linga!

Dissolving my mind in the Great Principle, you disappeared, O Basavanna, made one with the Absolute!

When, feeding with the grace that was bestowed and left, and giving her a form, you lodged mother Nāgāyi (his mother, Basavanna's sister) in your heart, my mind dissolved and swooned within your feet!

O Sangana Basavanna, that you may be the carrier of the purest Light to Kudala Chenna-Saṅgayya, you have become the Impartite!

Maḍivāḷa Māchayya eulogizes Basavanna in many vachanas. Vachana 74 on page 450 in volume V of Shunya Sampadane (1) is as follows:

The form has changed to Formlessness, Basavanna!
The breath has changed to Breathlessness, Basavanna!
They are over – your love and services to Linga and Jangama, Basavanna!
Silence has seized on you, Basavanna!

Entering the lotus of the heart of Kalidēva Deva, you have gone, a god to gods, Sangana Basavanna!

Then Maḍivāḷa Māchayya, on the occasion on which the innumerable Saints including Chennabasavanna attained the Absolute Void in the Great House of Ulavi, says *'the Grace of what was given and left by all the Saints has come to me'.* And then, Maḍivāḷa Māchayya attains unitive Void.

Here, Shūnya Saṁpādane implies that Maḍivāḷa Māchayya attains his unitive state also at Uḷuve, but elsewhere it is said that the unitive state of Maḍivāḷa Māchayya occurs at his birth place, not at Uḷuve.

Chennabasavanna attains his unitive state in the Void at Uḷuve (Ulavi). His vachana is the last vachana in Shunya Sampadane. It is as follows:

Unto the city extending wide twelve leagues,
Kalyana was the saucer lamp,
Therein the oil of Intellect was poured, and
As the flame of Knowledge was enkindled,
There was a blaze.

There everyone, with Kalayya, Choudayya, Kola Shantayya, Keshiraja of Mogavada, Khandeya Bommaṇṇa, Minda Mallinatha, Haḍapada Appaṇṇa, Maḍivāḷayya, Mother Nāgāyi, made one with Sangana Basavanna's end, went on.

Therefore, in Kudala Chenna-Sangama Deva, the end arrived for me as a Prasāda of these all.

There are 79 vachanas in this last chapter. The above Chennabasavanna's vachana is the last vachana in Shunya Sampadane.

Thus, Shunya Sampadane with its mystic discourses, ends auspiciously with vachana number 1,543.

Om! Shāntiḥ! Shāntiḥ! Shāntiḥ!

CONCLUDING REMARKS IN SHUNYA SAMPADANE

At the end of Shunya Sampadane, after chapter twenty-one, the composer of Shunya Sampadane Sri Gūḷūra Siddhavīraṇārya gives his concluding remarks. First he lists nine statements, and then he narrates his comments.

The list of nine statements is the same as that given at the beginning of this book. It has been give twice in this book because of its profound impact on the philosophy and the practice concepts of the Veerashaivas.

Shunya Sampadane gives this list of statements:

- This is the best guide, the philosophical system of exalted Veerashaiva doctrine.
- This is that which expounds and firmly establishes the Veerashaiva practice.
- This is the crest-jewel of the divine Vedanta.
- This is the chief mirror of all the sciences.
- This is the teaching of the highest Experience to promote the Supreme Knowledge.
- This is a catalogue of those who, endowed with all kinds of religious practice, have attained the Height.
- This is a treasury of the attainment of the great Raja yoga.

- This is a happy feast of the ambrosial essence of Existence-Consciousness-Bliss, eternal and perfect.
- This is a great conference of Prabhudeva on the attainment of Shunya – an instrument to remove ignorance.

Shunya Sampadane is the main scripture of the Veerashaivas.

Then Śrī Gūḷūra Siddhavīraṇārya makes his remarks. The remarks include the statement saying that the Sharaṇas of Shiva should listen to Shūnya Saṁpādane, cherish it, and write and read it.

At the end there are four stanzas, the last one is as follows:

Siddhavīrayōgīshvara,
He who set firmly in his heart
The lotus feet of Guru Tōṇṭada Siddhēsha,
Imparted this wisdom of the vachanas
To the Sharaṇa's ears.

This is the end of Prabhudēva's Shūnya Saṁpādane.

Great auspices!

Śrī. Śrī. Śrī. Śrī. Śrī.

Ōṁ

REFERENCES

1. ŚŪNYASAṀPĀDANE. Volumes I through V. Published by Karnataka University, Dharwad, India.

2. VEERASHAIVIM [VĪRAŚAIVISM] Fifth Edition. Hard-cover print book ISBN: 9798761040151. Also soft-cover print book ISBN: 9798772606612. Linga Raju amazon.com November 2021.

3. Gaṇaka Vachana Saṁpuṭa from taralabalu.org web-site. Sri Taraḷabāḷu Jagadguru Brihanmaṭh, Sirigere, Karnataka, India.

4. GODS, SAGES AND KINGS. Vedic Secrets of Ancient Civilization, by David Frawley. Passage Press, Morison Publishing, P. O. Box 21713, Salt Lake City, Utah 84121, USA. 1991

5. THE BHAGAVAD GITA with Sanskrit Text. Translation by Swami Chidbhavananda. Published by The Secretary, Sri Ramakrishna Tapovanam. Tirupparaitturai, India. 1976

6. Shri Shivayogi Shivāchārya's Shri Siddhāntaśikhāmaṇi with Shri Maritoṇṭadārya's Tattvapradīpikā. Dr. M. Sivakumara Swamy. Shaiva Bharati Shodha Pratisthāna, Jaṅgamwadi Math, Varanasi-221 001, India. 2007

7. ISHAVASYOPANISHAD by Swami Śarvānanda. Sri Ramakrishna Math, Madras 600 004, India. 2007

8. THE BRIHADARANYAKA UPANISHAD Sri Ramakrishna Math, Mylapore, Chennai 4, India. 2004

9. SHVETASHVATAROPANISHAD by Swami Tyagishananda. Sri Ramakrishna Math, Mylapore, Chennai 4, India. 2006

10. KATHHOPANISHAD by Swami Sharvananda. Sri Ramakrishna Math, 16 Ramakrishna Math Road, Madras 600 004, India. 2007

11. RIGVEDA SAMHITA according to the translation of H. H. Wilson, and Bhashya of Sayanacharya, volumes I through IV. Ravi Prakash Arya, K. L. Joshi. Primal Publications. Indica Books, D 40/18 Godowlia, Varanasi 221 001, India. 2002

12. The Rig Veda. Complete. Translated by Ralph T. H, Griffith. Republished 2008 by Forgotten Books

13. CHĀNDOGYA UPANISHAD by Swami Swahananda. Sri Ramakrishna Math, Mylapore, Chennai (Madras) 600 004, India. 2007

14. Evolution of Veerashaiva Concepts. Fifth Edition in paperback print book. ISBN: 9781520848709 Linga Raju amazon.com Updated 2020.

15. 112 UPANISHADS (Sanskrit Text, English Translation, an Exhaustive Introduction & Index of Verses). In two volumes. Translated By Board of Scholars. Edited & Revised By K. L. Joshi, O. N.

Bimali. Bindiya Trivedi. Primal Publications, Delhi, India. Third thoroughly Revised Edition: 2007

16. KENOPANISHAD by Swami Sharvananda. Sri Ramakrishna Math, Mylapore, Chennai 4, India. 2007

17. MANDUKYOPANISHAD by Swami Sarvananda. Sri Ramakrishna Math, Mylapore, Chennai 4, India. 2004

18. PRASHNOPANISHAD by Swami Sharvananda. Sri Ramakrishna Math, 16 Ramakrishna Math Road, Madras 600 004, India. 2005

19. YOGA for the Beginners. Swami Gnaneswarananda. Edited and Compiled by Mallika Clare Gupta. Sri Ramakrishna Math, Mylapore, Madras, India. Fifth Impression.

20. MUNDAKOPANISHAD by Swami Sarvananda. Sri Ramakrishna Math, Mylapore, Madras 600 004, India. 2001

21. TAITTIRIYOPANISHAD by Swami Sarvananda. Sri Ramakrishna Math, Mylapore, Chennai 4, India. 2008

22. AITAREYOPANISAD by Swami Sharvananda. Sri Ramakrishna Math, Mylapore, Chennai 4, India. 2005

23. SHANKARA'S ADVAITA by R. D. Karmarkar. October 1966. Karnataka University, Dharwad, Karnataka, India.

24. The Vedas. Sri Chandrasekharendra Saraswati, Bhavan's Book University, Bharatiya Vidya Bhavan, Mumbai, India. Eighth Edition 2009.

25. SAMAVEDA SAMHITA, Sanskrit Text with English Translation of R. T. H. Griffith, Edited and revised with an introduction and exegical notes by Ravi Prakash Arya. Primal Publications, 27/28 Shakti Nagar, Delhi – 110007, India. Second Revised Edition 2003

26. YAJURVEDA SAMHITA (SHUKLA), Sanskrit Text with English Translation by R. T. H. Griffith, Edited and revised with an introduction and exegical notes by Ravi Prakash Arya. Primal Publications India Books, D 40/18 Godowlia, Varanasi – 221 001 (UP), India. 2002

27. IN SEARCH OF THE CRADLE OF CIVILIZATION. New Light on Ancient India. Georg Feuerstein, Subhash Kak and David Frawley. Motilal Banarsidass Publishers, Delhi, India. This Edition reproduced from Quest Books 2001 Edition.

28. Essence of the Vachanas. The Twelfth Century Sharana Philosophy and Practice. Linga Raju. ISBN: 9781522005001 paperback print book (307 pages) at amazon.com web-site. 2017

29. Spiritual Spouse Akka Mahadevi. Linga Raju. ISBN: 9781549688973 paperback print book (170 pages) at amazon.com web-site. 2017